WORCESTER TO HEREFORD

including the branches to Leominster and Gloucester

Vic Mitchell and Keith Smith

Middleton Press

Cover picture: Approaching Ledbury with the 8.35am train from Cardiff to Birmingham on 23rd August 1954 is no. 6992 Aborfield Hall. *Its injector is overflowing onto the points of the line from Gloucester. (H.C.Casserley)*

Published August 2004

ISBN 1 904474 38 1

© Middleton Press, 2004

Design   Deborah Esher
            David Pede

Published by
            Middleton Press
            Easebourne Lane
            Midhurst, West Sussex
            GU29 9AZ
Tel: 01730 813169
Fax: 01730 812601
Email: info@middletonpress.co.uk
www.middletonpress.co.uk

Printed & bound by Biddles Ltd, Kings Lynn

CONTENTS

1	Worcester Foregate Street to Bransford Road Junction	1- 14
2	Leigh Court to Leominster	15- 42
3	Bransford Road to Ledbury	43- 79
4	Ledbury to Gloucester	80-101
5	Ashperton to Hereford	102-120

ACKNOWLEDGEMENTS

We are very grateful for the assistance received from many of those mentioned in the credits and also to P.G.Barnes, A.E.Bennett, L.Crosier, G.Croughton, S.P.Derek, G.Heathcliffe, F.Jeanes, N.Langridge, J.S.Petley, D.T.Rowe, Mr D. and Dr S.Salter, Dr R.Willé and particularly our ever supportive wives, Barbara Mitchell and Janet Smith.

I. Location map - 1947 (Railway Clearing House)

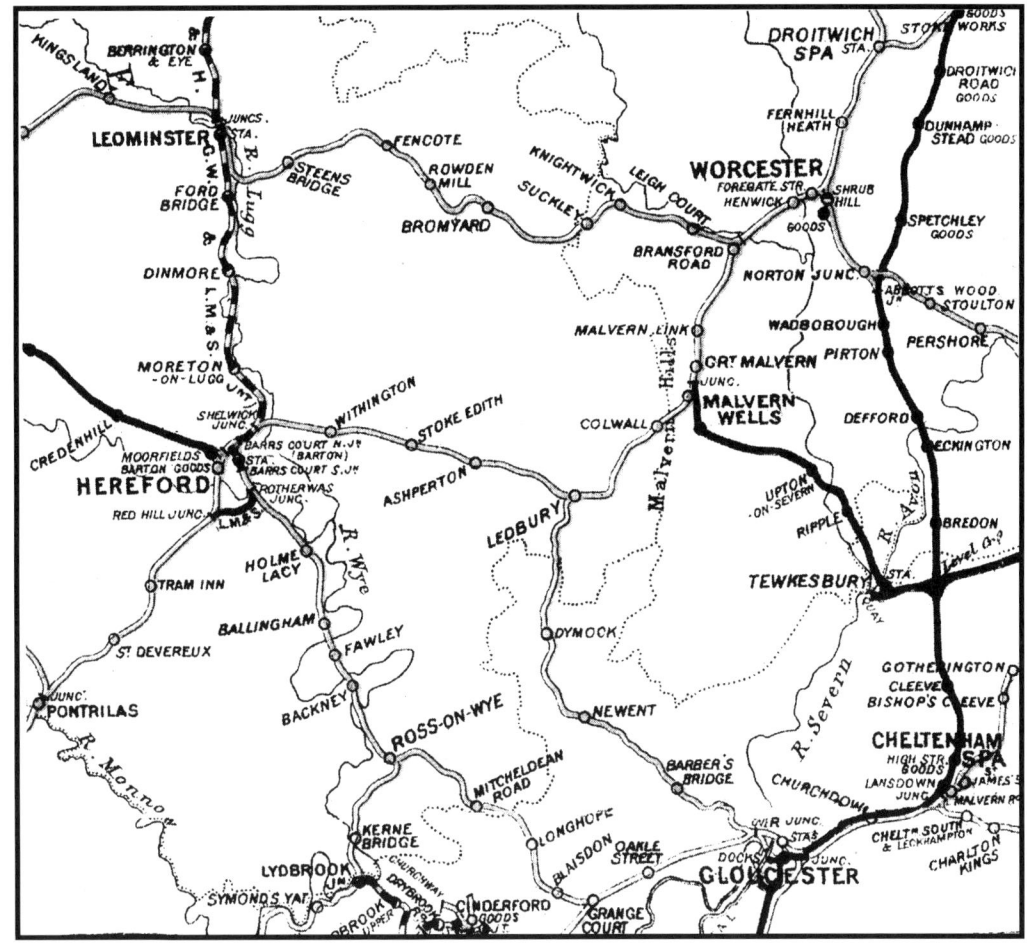

INDEX

102	Ashperton	9	Henwick	46	Newland Halt
95	Barbers Bridge	112	Hereford	97	Over Junction
43	Bransford Road	19	Knightwick	32	Rowden Mill
13	Bransford Road Junction	70	Ledbury	12	Rushwick Halt
27	Bromyard	80	Ledbury Town Halt	110	Shelwick Junction
65	Colwall	15	Leigh Court	37	Steens Bridge
84	Dymock	40	Leominster	104	Stoke Edith
34	Fencote	93	Malswick Halt	39	Stoke Prior Halt
87	Four Oaks Halt	48	Malvern Link	22	Suckley
99	Gloucester	61	Malvern Wells	108	Withington
51	Great Malvern	89	Newent	1	Worcester Foregate St.
82	Greenway Halt				

GEOGRAPHICAL SETTING

Our journey begins close to the River Severn in the ancient City of Worcester and will soon pass over a notable tributary, the River Teme. A steady climb ensues for three miles over mainly Marl before reaching the foot of the Malvern Hills. This impressive outcrop of ancient hard rocks is an outlier of the Welsh mountains. This necessitates a continuation of the climb for a further four miles before the ridge is penetrated in Colwall Tunnel.

A steady descent to the Leadon Valley, one mile west of Ledbury, takes the line onto fairly level Old Red Sandstone for the journey to the long established City of Hereford, an important market centre. Hop gardens and orchards are numerous.

The route to Leominster follows the Teme Valley for about four miles and then climbs steeply to Bromyard. Gradients of up to 1 in 44 are encountered before reaching the summit at Fencote. A long descent follows into the valley of the River Lugg at Leominster, usually pronounced Lem-ster. (Most places ending with "wick", on these lines, have a silent W.)

The Ledbury branch to Gloucester runs down the Leadon Valley to Dymock after which it climbs over a ridge to rejoin the river on its way towards the Severn, just west of Gloucester. This is the third county town to be featured in this album.

The maps are to the scale of 25 ins to 1 mile, with north at the top, unless otherwise indicated.

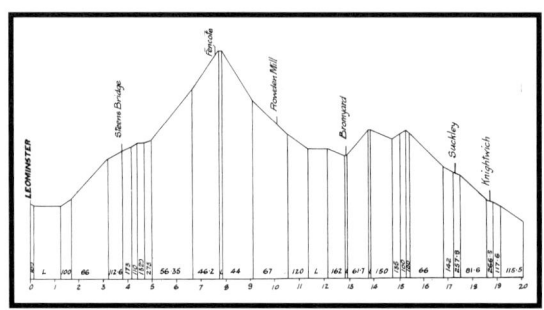

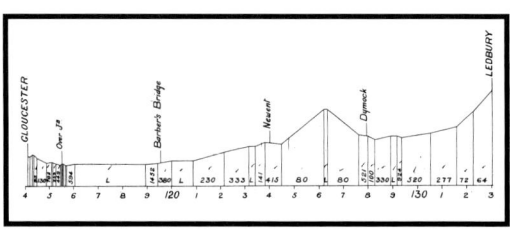

HISTORICAL BACKGROUND

The Act for a Worcester & Hereford Railway was passed in 1853, but it was to be 1856 before the scheme was moved forward by the joint action of the Oxford, Worcester & Wolverhampton Railway and the Newport, Abergavenny & Hereford Railway. The former had reached Worcester in 1852 when its Droitwich - Evesham section came into use, although the first trains to that city had arrived in 1850 on a branch operated by the Midland Railway.

Hereford's initial service was from the north when the route opened from Shrewsbury in 1853. It became a joint line under the control of the Great Western Railway and the London & North Western Railway.

The NAHR was completed to Hereford in 1854 and it, together with the OWWR, became part of the GWR, as did the 1855 line from Ross-on-Wye. The Midland Railway eventually operated the route west of Hereford, this opening in 1863.

The Worcester-Hereford section opened in stages: from Henwick to Malvern Link on 25th July 1859, Worcester Shrub Hill to Henwick and Malvern Link to Malvern Wells on 17th May 1860. The triangle at Worcester was completed in July 1860 and in the same month the OWWR absorbed the WHR and the NAHR, the new group being known as the West Midlands Railway. A single line from Malvern Wells to Shelwick Junction enabled trains to reach Hereford from 13th September 1861, using the tracks of the Shrewsbury & Hereford Railway. Doubling was completed by 1868, but the tunnels always remained single. The WMR had become part of the GWR in 1863.

Malvern Wells had two stations from 16th May 1864, when the MR route from Tewkesbury came into use. The Worcester - Leominster line was opened in stages: to Knightwick on 2nd May 1874 and to Bromyard on 22nd October 1877. The Steens Bridge - Leominster section had trains from 1st March 1884, but the Bromyard - Steens Bridge part had to wait until 1st September 1897 for the final link. The entire route was single track between the junctions. (A temporary terminus at Yearsett, between Suckley and Bromyard, was in use in 1874-77).

Services between Ledbury and Gloucester began on 27th July 1885 and were operated by the GWR. The final part of the journey between Over Junction and Gloucester was on the main line which had been opened by the South Wales Railway in 1851. The first line to that city had been completed from Birmingham in 1840.

Upon nationalisation in 1948, all the routes became part of the Western Region of British Railways and passenger services were withdrawn from the lines featured in this album thus: Bromyard to Leominster on 15th September 1952, Ledbury to Gloucester on 13th July 1959 and Worcester to Bromyard on 7th September 1964. Closure of goods depots and main line intermediate stations are detailed in the captions.

Privatisation resulted in London services being provided by Thames Trains from 13th October 1996. This franchise was transferred to First Great Western Link on 1st April 2004. Birmingham services over the route were operated by Central Trains from 2nd March 1997.

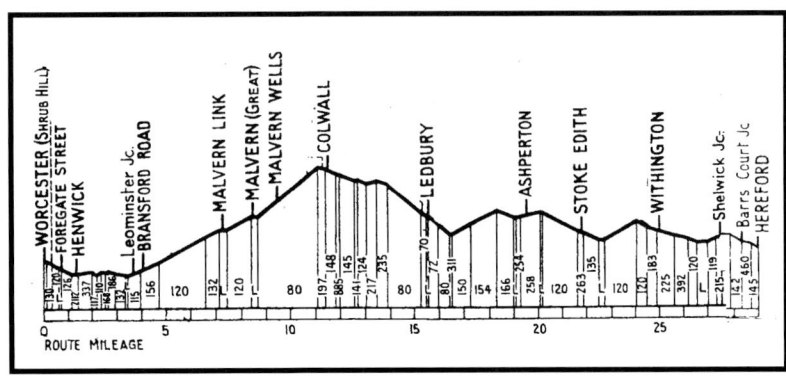

PASSENGER SERVICES

The isolated section between Henwick and Malvern Link was provided with nine trains on weekdays and eight on Sundays. Passengers were allowed to walk over the incomplete bridge over the River Severn at Worcester for nine months.

The figures given are for trains running the full length of the route; there were many short workings south as far as one of the Malvern stations or Colwall. Only trains running on at least five days per week are included.

	Weekdays	Sundays
1869	6	2
1889	3	1
1901	6	1
1921	10	1
1941	13	3
1961	14	9
1981	16	6
2001	20	8

The Midland Railway also operated four fast trains over the route between 1st July 1869 and 31st October 1872. Thereafter, through coaches between Birmingham and Swansea were attached to GWR trains until 1916.

Bromyard branch

Initially there were four trains, weekdays only, to Yearsett and the same frequency was maintained upon extension to Bromyard. The service between Steens Bridge and Leominster was identical. Following completion of the route in 1897, five trains were provided until Sunday trains were run to the south of Bromyard in some Summers from 1923. In its final years, the branch had only three trains weekdays only.

Ledbury branch

The route to Gloucester had four or five trains each weekday until its final years, when the figure was reduced to three. We found no record of Sunday trains in the years sampled.

September 1925

September 1925

January 1945

GLOUCESTER and LEDBURY

(Third class only. Limited accommodation.)

Miles	Down	Week Days only. mrn	mrn		mrn	aft E	aft S	
	74 London (Pad.)...dep	12 55	5 30	..	10H45	1 55	4 15	..
—	Gloucester .... dep	7 0	9 55	..	3 55	7 0	7 35	..
5½	Barber's Bridge ¶......	7 12	10 7	..	4 7	7 12	7 47	..
10	Newent ¶................	7 25	10 20	..	4 19	7 25	8 0	..
13¾	Dymock ¶...............	7 37	10 32	..	4 31	7 38	8 12	..
19	Ledbury 122, 125 ... arr	7 52	10 50	..	4 46	7 53	8 33	..
32¾	122 HEREFORD .... arr	8 40	11 56	..	5 58	8 56	8 56	..
26	125 MALVERN (Great) "	8 32	11 39	..	5 21	9 30	9 30	..
34½	125 WORCESTER (S.H.) "	8F51	12 0	..	5 40	9 50	9 50	..

Miles	Up	Week Days only. mrn	mrn		aft	aft	
	122 WORCESTER (S.H.) dep	7 15	1035	..	3 15	7 52	..
	122 MALVERN (Great) "	7 44	11 3	..	3 45	8 20	..
	125 HEREFORD .... "	7 40	1045	..	4 30	7 15	..
—	Ledbury ¶..........dep	8 18	1135	..	5 10	8 55	..
5¼	Dymock ¶...............	8 31	1150	..	5 23	9 9	..
9	Newent ¶................	8 41	12 1	..	5 33	9 20	.
13½	Barber's Bridge...[128	8 52	1213	..	5 45	9 30	..
19	Gloucester 74, 75, 76 arr	9 4	1225	..	5 58	9 43	..
133	75 London (Pad.)...arr	1245	8 10	..	11 10	5Z10	..

E Except Saturdays. F Foregate Street. H Dep 12 5 aft on Sats S Saturdays only. Z mrn.
¶ "Halts" at Malswick, between Barber's Bridge and Newent; at Four Oaks, between Newent and Dymock; at Greenway and at Ledbury Town between Dymock and Ledbury.

January 1945

GLOUCESTER and LEDBURY

WEEK DAYS ONLY—(Second class only)

Miles		am	Saturdays only am	pm	pm	
	105 London (Paddington).. dep	..	7 30	11C45	2 15	..
—	**Gloucester Central** .... dep	6 42	12p10	4 8	6 24	....
5½	Barber's Bridge..	6 53	12 21	4 19	6 38	..
8½	Malswick Halt	7 1	12 29	4 27	6 47	....
10	Newent	7 5	12 35	4 32	6 52	..
12	Four Oaks Halt..............	7 11	12 40	4 38	6 58	....
13¾	Dymock	7 16	12 45	4 45	7 4	..
15¼	Greenway Halt	7 21	12 50	4 49	7 8	....
18¼	Ledbury Town Halt..	7 28	12 58	4 56	7 16	..
19	**Ledbury** .... arr	7 32	1 1	5 0	7 19	....
32¾	164 Hereford .. .. .. arr	8 37	1 46	6 10	8 30	..
26	164 Great Malvern........ "	8 9	1 30	5 52	8A 5	....
34½	164 Worcester (Foregate St) "	8 26	1 45	6 5	8A20	..

Miles		am	Saturdays only pm	pm	pm	
	164 Worcester (Foregate St) dep	..	12 47	3 30	7 32	..
	164 Great Malvern........ "	....	1 3	3 56	7 48	....
	164 Hereford .. .. .. "	7 20	12 55	4 28	6 55	..
—	**Ledbury** .... dep	7 55	1 30	5 25	8 22	....
¾	Ledbury Town Halt..	7 57	1 32	5 27	8 24	..
3¾	Greenway Halt	8 5	1 40	5 34	8 3[illegible]	....
5¼	Dymock	8 9	1 44	5 39	8 40	..
7	Four Oaks Halt..............	8 13	1 48	5 44	8 46	....
9	Newent	8 18	1 53	5 50	8 52	..
10½	Malswick Halt	8 22	1 56	5 54	....	....
13½	Barber's Bridge..	8 30	2 4	6 2	9 2	..
19	**Gloucester Central** .... arr	8 42	2 17	6 16	9 15	....
133	105 London (Paddington).. arr	12B25	5 40	10 10	..	..

A On Saturdays arr Great Malvern 8 47 pm, Worcester (Foregate St.) 9 1 pm B On Saturdays arr 12 35 pm
C am. Via Kingham and Cheltenham Spa (Malvern Rd.) p pm

June - September 1959

1963 - 1964

WORCESTER, KNIGHTWICK and BROMYARD

WEEK DAYS ONLY—(Second class only)

Miles		Saturdays only A am		pm T		pm		pm		Saturdays only pm				
—	**Worcester** (S. Hill).. dep	9 38	..	1 5	..	4 10	..	5 45	..	1015	..	..	..	..
¾	" (Foregate St.) dep	9 43	....	1 10	....	4J23	....	5 51	....	1019	....	....	....	....
1¼	Henwick	9 46	..	..	..	4 26	..	5 54	..	..	..	..	..	..
2½	Rushwick Halt...........	....	....	....	....	....	....	5 57	....	....	....	....	....	....
5½	Leigh Court	9 57	..	1 20	..	4 35	..	6 6	..	1033	..	..	..	..
8½	Knightwick	10 4	....	1 28	....	4 42	....	6 13	....	1040	....	....	....	....
10	Suckley	10 9	..	1 33	..	4 47	..	6 18	..	1045	..	..	..	..
14½	**Bromyard** .... arr	1020	....	1 44	....	4 58	....	6 29	....	1056	....	....	....	....

Miles		am		Saturdays only A am		pm T		pm		pm		Saturdays only pm			
—	**Bromyard** .. .. dep	7 40	..	1050	..	1 56	..	5 15	..	6 50	..	11 5	..	..	..
4½	Suckley	7 54	....	11 1	....	2 7	....	5 27	....	7 1	....	1116	....	....	....
6	Knightwick	7 58	..	11 6	..	2 12	..	5 33	..	7 5	..	1122	..	..	..
9	Leigh Court.............	8 5	....	1112	....	2 19	....	5 39	....	7 13	....	1130	....	....	....
12	Rushwick Halt	8 13	..	..	..	..	..	..	..	..	..	..	..	..	..
13¼	Henwick................	8 17	....	1123	....	2 30	....	5 50	....	....	....	....	....	....	....
13¾	**Worcester** arr	8 19	..	1125	..	2 32	..	5 52	..	7 24	..	1145	..	..	..
	(Foregate St.) dep	8 22	....	1126	....	2 33	....	5 53	....	7 26	....	....	....	....	....
14½	" (S. Hill).. arr	8 25	..	1129	..	2 38	..	5 56	..	7 29	..	..	..	..	..

A First and second class
J Arr 4 15 pm
T Thursdays and Saturdays only

A Birmingham and Midland Motor Omnibus leaves Newport Street Worcester daily at 8 3 pm and through ordinary railway ticket holders for Knightwick and Bromyard may travel by this bus. Hand luggage only conveyed. Rail tickets must be exchanged for Omnibus permits at either Worcester (Shrub Hill) or Worcester (Foregate Street) Station Booking Office

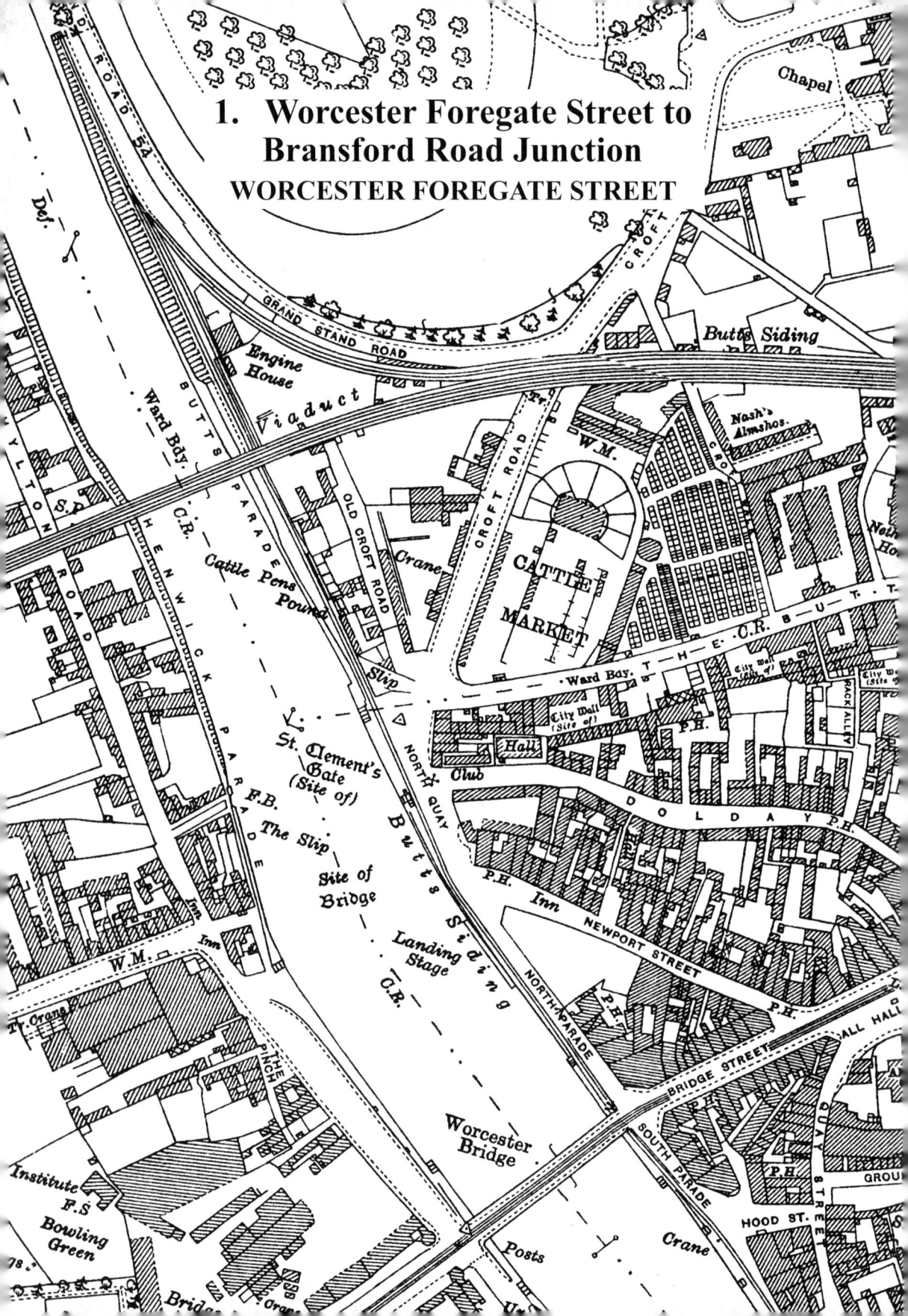
1. Worcester Foregate Street to Bransford Road Junction
WORCESTER FOREGATE STREET

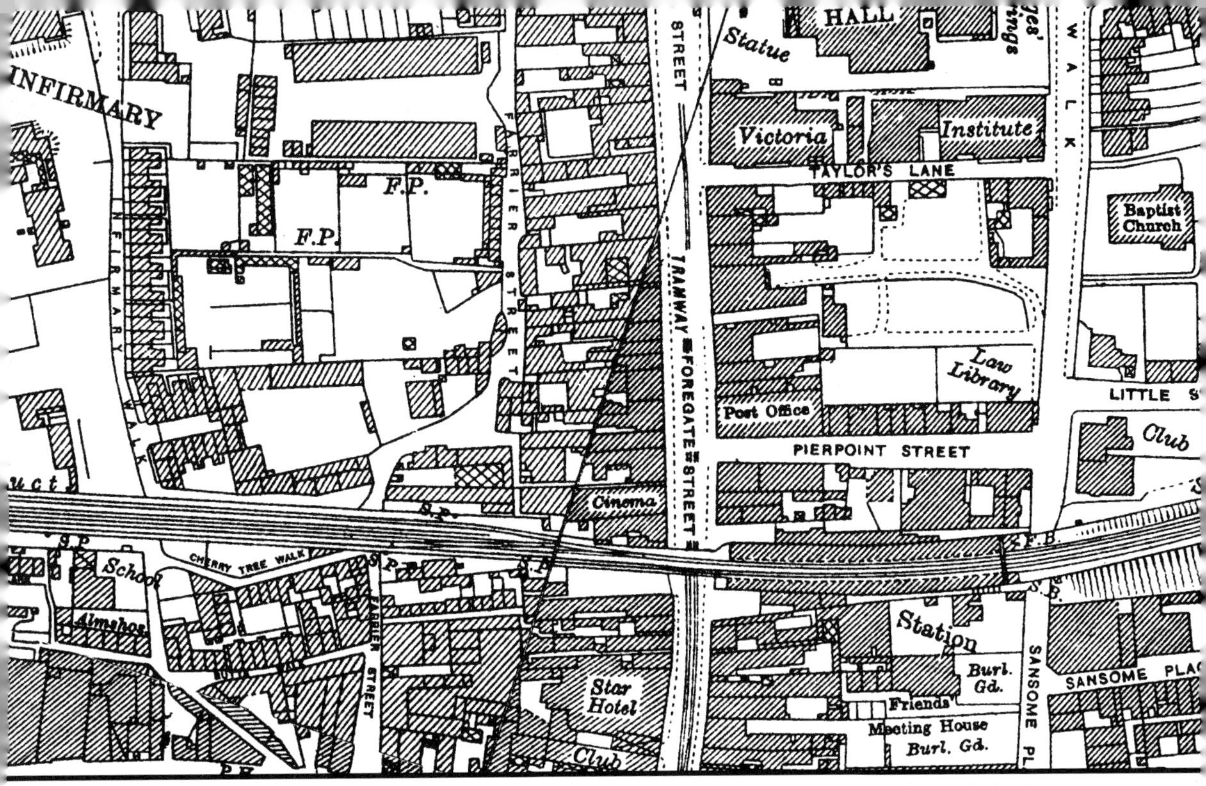

II.   Few stations are so well situated to a city centre as this one. Shrub Hill is relatively remote and is featured in our *Moreton-in-Marsh to Worcester* album. This 1928 extract includes almost all of Butts Siding, which begins near the station (right) and descends steeply beside the main line and curves close to the racecourse. It then returns along the quays of the River Severn, but this section was lifted in the early 1930s; the rest followed in 1957. The "Engine House" contained the GWR's pumping engine and nearby was a platform for horseboxes, this closing on 25th April 1953. All traffic ceased in 1955, but the branch viaduct can still be seen. It is 553yds long.

1.   A view towards Hereford in the days of gas lighting includes the steps to the signal box. There were no goods facilities at this station. (D.Symonds coll.)

2. Looking in the other direction, it becomes apparent that the footbridge was adjacent to the signal box. (D.Symonds coll.)

3. The entrance was photographed in 1960, along with the 1909 bridge which bears the GWR arms flanked by those of the City of Worcester. Trams were operated by the Worcester Electric Traction Company from 1904-1928, one route passing under this bridge. (M.A.N.Johnston)

4.　　A photo from 4th November 1961 includes a train from Bromyard and the 23-lever signal box, which had closed on 16th August 1959. (E.Wilmshurst)

5.　　Rationalisation on 21st November 1973 meant that both tracks became single lines east of Henwick, with Birmingham services using platform 2 (ignore the blind) and Shrub Hill trains calling at no.1. A class 115 DMU is seen on 3rd August 1989. (M.Turvey)

6. Class 170 Turbostars were introduced in 1998 and this 3-car unit of Central Trains was working the 12.45 Hereford to Nottingham service on 26th March 2003. (V.Mitchell)

7. The entire station was built on brick arches and is seen on the same day from Foregate Street bridge. On the right is a former signal box which was in use as a buffet. (V.Mitchell)

WEST OF WORCESTER FOREGATE STREET

8. The viaduct is 935yds in length and includes 68 brick arches, the Forgate Street girders and these graceful lattice spans. They replaced the original 1860 two-arch bridge in 1905. During the disastrous floods of March 1947, Worcester was cut in two by the River Severn, which rose to 17ft above normal. The only way across was by train, and the Great Western instituted an emergency railcar service between Foregate Street and Henwick, running every 15 minutes, on each of the four days of the emergency. (T.Heavyside)

HENWICK

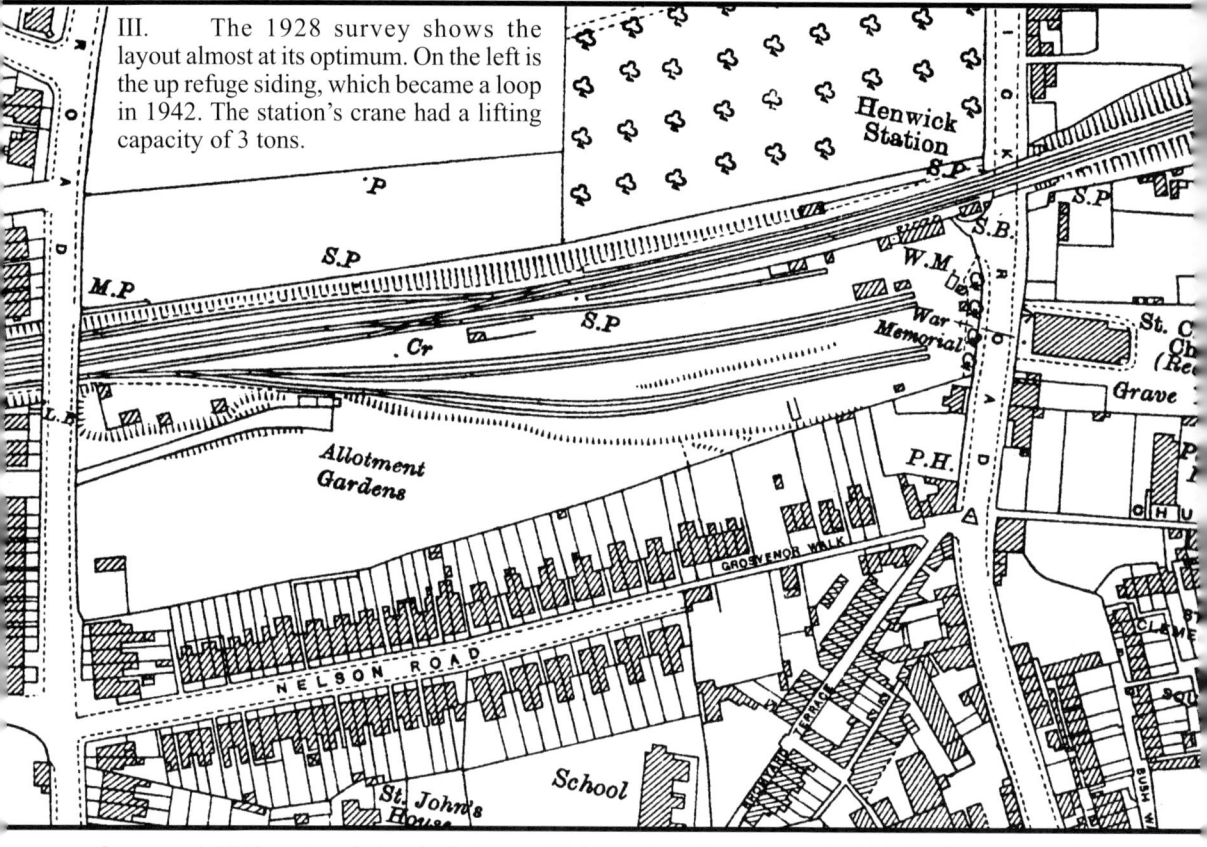

III. The 1928 survey shows the layout almost at its optimum. On the left is the up refuge siding, which became a loop in 1942. The station's crane had a lifting capacity of 3 tons.

9. A 1919 eastward view includes the 25-lever signal box, beyond which St. Clements siding was added for Worcester Corporation for the purpose of providing coal to the power station. It was in place until 1968. (LGRP/NRM)

10. Looking west in about 1960, we witness shunting in the goods yard, which closed on 1st May 1968. There had been a siding for the Mining Engineering Company beyond the bridge. (Lens of Sutton coll.)

11. Passenger service ceased on 5th April 1965 and all except the signal box was removed. It was retained to control the full lifting barriers (installed in November 1971) and two crossovers (one behind the camera), which are at the west end of the two single lines seen in picture 7. The up refuge siding was still in place, two of the point rods serving it. The photo is from 2003. (V.Mitchell)

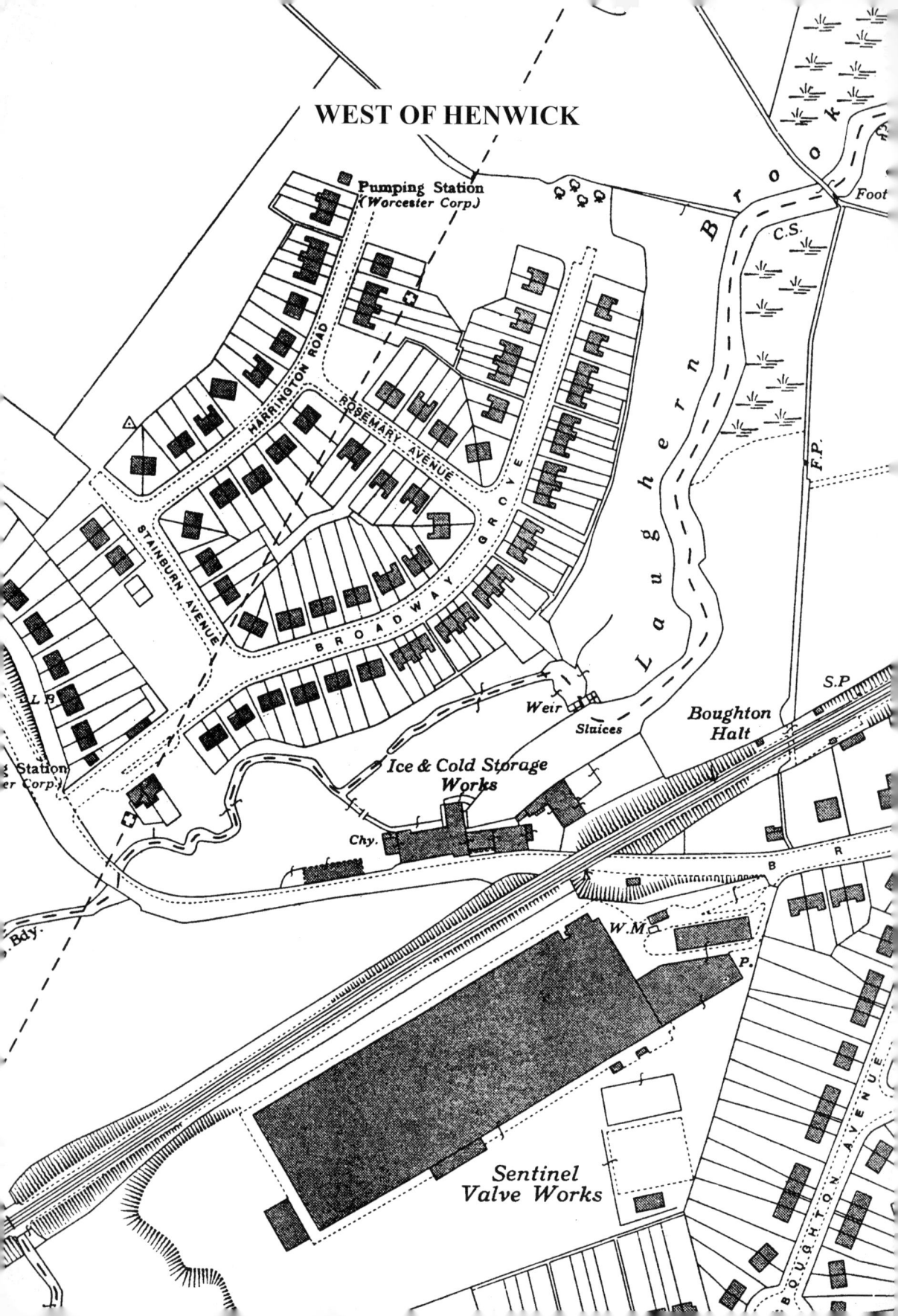

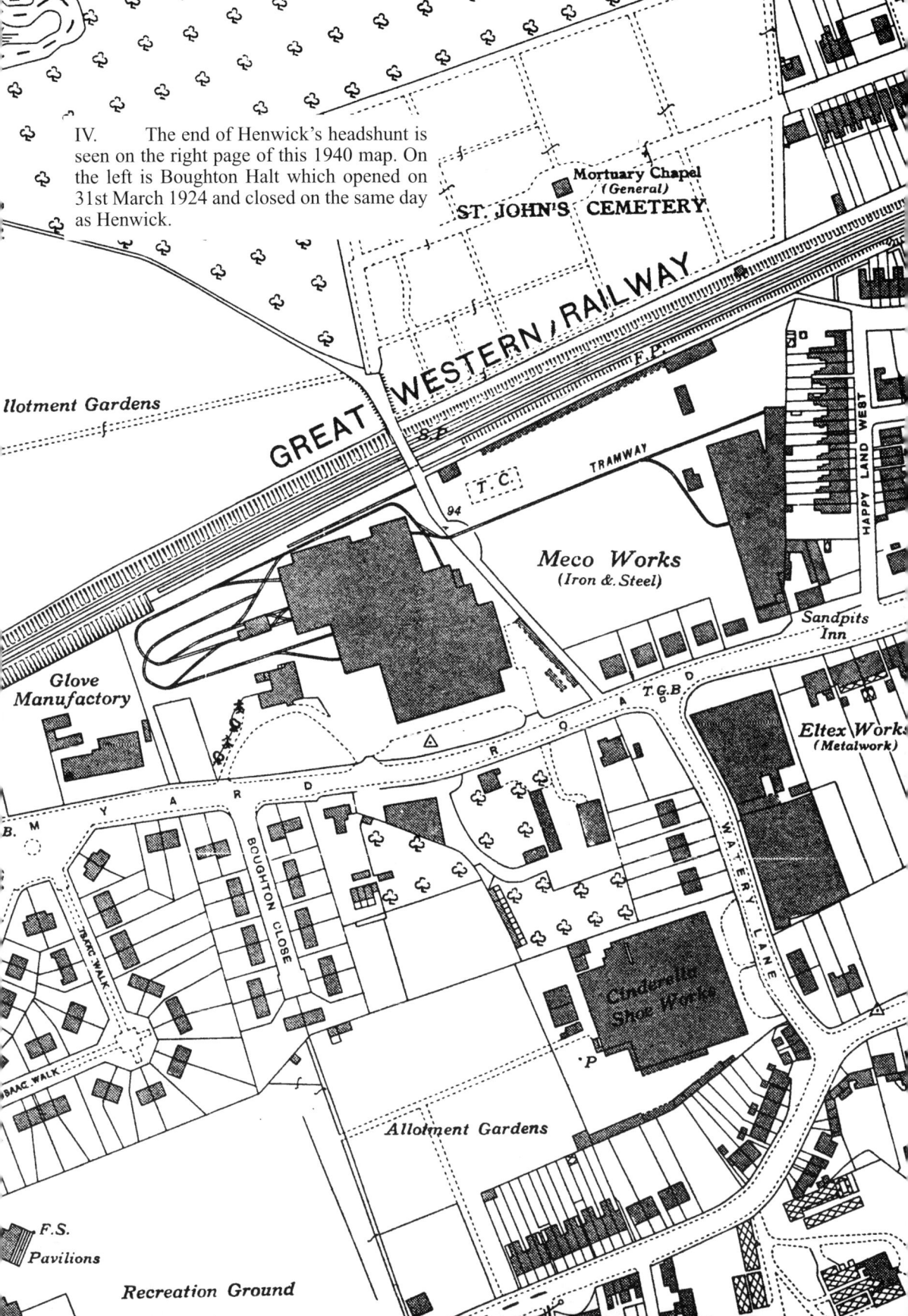

IV. The end of Henwick's headshunt is seen on the right page of this 1940 map. On the left is Boughton Halt which opened on 31st March 1924 and closed on the same day as Henwick.

RUSHWICK HALT

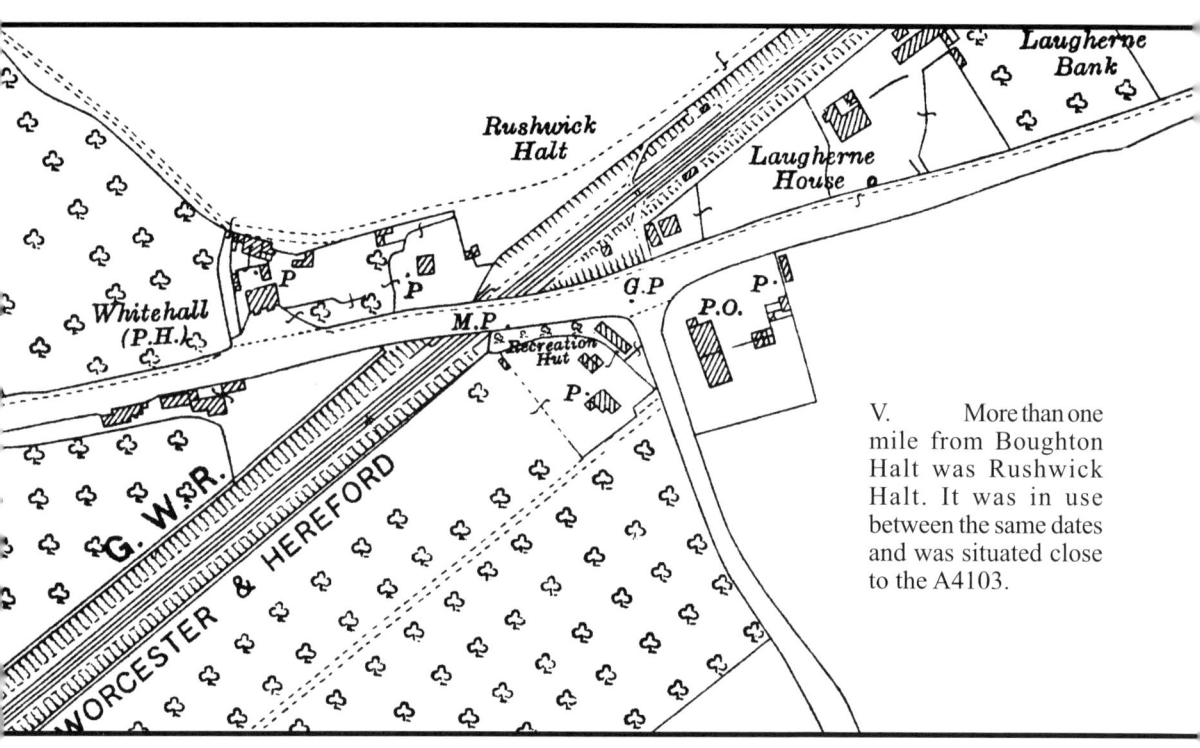

V. More than one mile from Boughton Halt was Rushwick Halt. It was in use between the same dates and was situated close to the A4103.

12. The halt was photographed in 1961, along with hop poles and the hoist for a pressurised oil lamp. Orchards were behind the camera. (Stations UK)

BRANSFORD ROAD JUNCTION

13. Two pictures from August 1959 show the complexity of the telephone and telegraph wiring. This panorama also includes part of the impressive Malvern Hills on the left. The name "Leominster Junction" was used from 1897 to 1950. (P.J.Garland/R.S.Carpenter)

14. The tablet is caught by the signalman as a train leaves the Bromyard branch. The white post would bear the tablet pouch and hoop prior to trains running onto the branch. The box had 20 levers and was in use from 10th May 1911 until 18th October 1964. (P.J.Garland/R.S.Carpenter)

2. Leigh Court to Leominster
LEIGH COURT

VI. This is the 1928 edition.

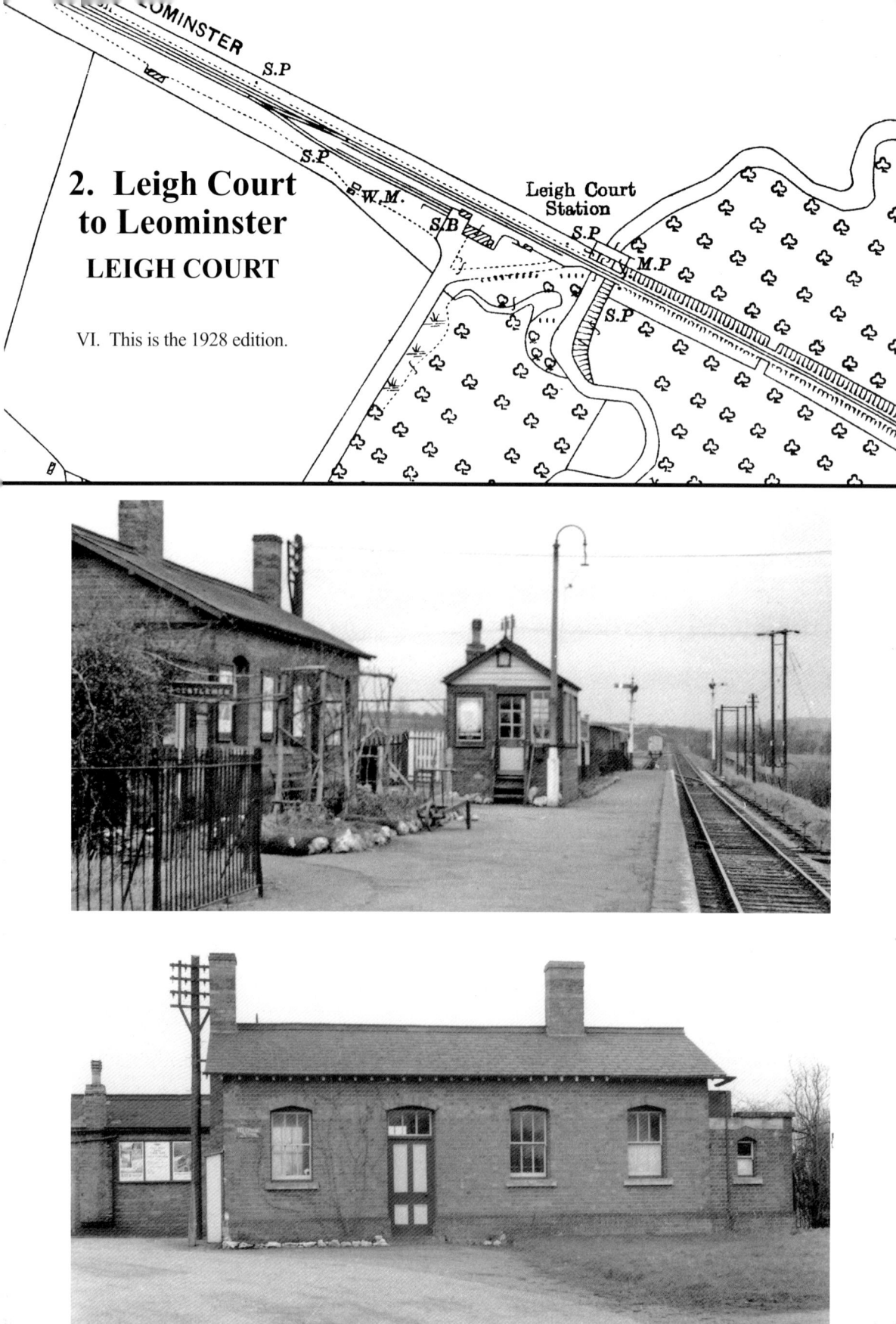

(left) 15. We can now enjoy two tranquil scenes from 1954. Two sidings and two signals are included, but the latter disappeared when the 11-lever signal box became a ground frame on 21st October 1956. (J.Moss/R.S.Carpenter)

(lower left) 16. A sign near the battery cupboard invites you to telephone from here; the operator would advise the cost at the end of the call. It seems that water was supplied from the roof gutter to a tank above the toilets. A hand pump was also available. (J.Moss/R.S.Carpenter)

17. An ex-GWR twin railcar was in use on 4th November 1961 when two passengers were on offer. The numbers of staff employed remained at a total of two between 1903 and 1938. (E.Wilmshurst)

18. Later in 1961, a single car was under observation by two local lads. "Worcester Shrub Hill" is displayed between the two exhaust pipes. All traffic ceased on 7th September 1964. (Stations UK)

KNIGHTWICK

19. This view is towards Worcester in 1954 and includes the goods shed. Three staff were employed at the station in 1903 which decreased to two employees by 1938. The crane was capable of lifting up to 1 ton 10 cwts. (J.Moss/R.S.Carpenter)

20. Looking in the same direction we see the level headshunt, with the running line dropping away beyond the ground frame. The siding on the far right was added in 1925. The box had an 11 lever frame but was not a block post. (J.Moss/R.S.Carpenter)

21.   A view towards Bromyard on 23rd April 1958 includes a water tank in the dock siding, with a Hillman Minx nearby. The population of the village was 168 in 1901. (R.M.Casserley)

VII.   The 1905 survey at 6 ins to 1 mile reveals the remote location of the station and the long road to the village.

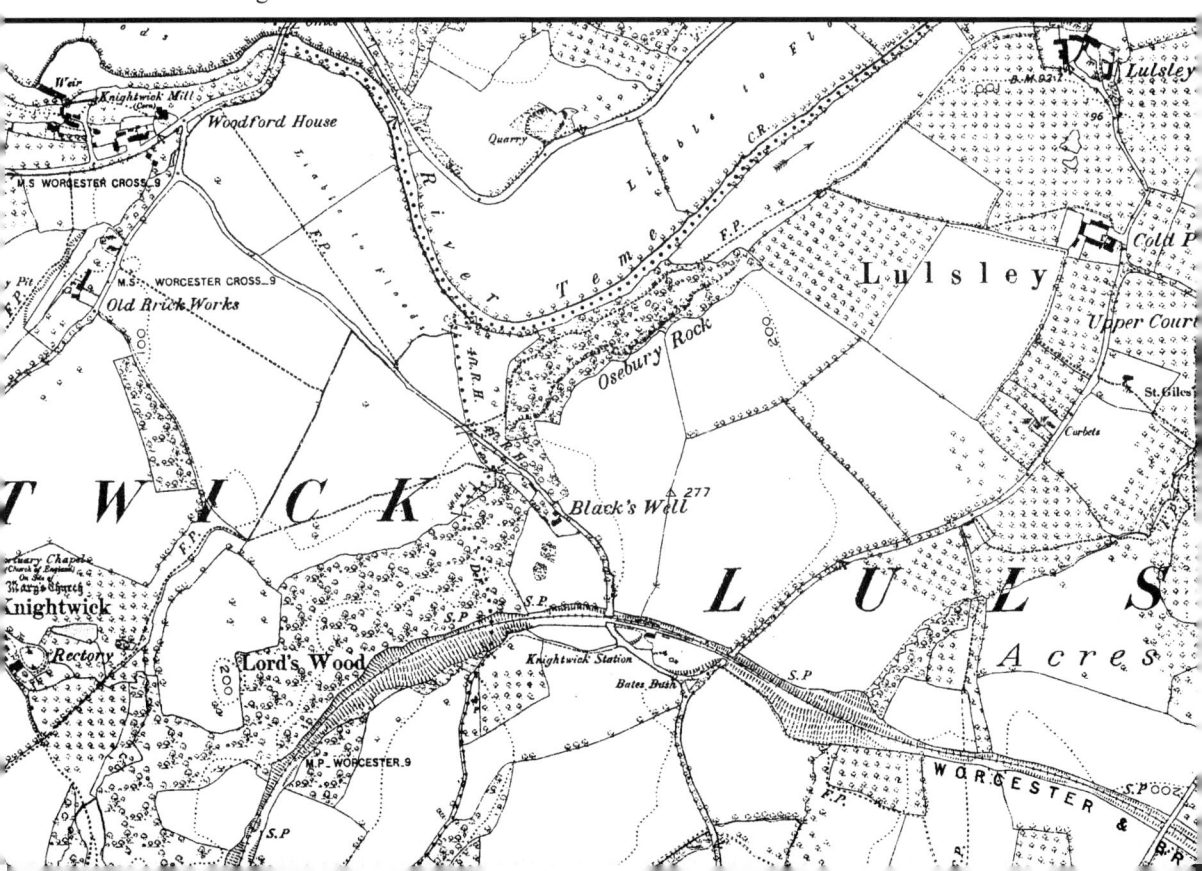

SUCKLEY

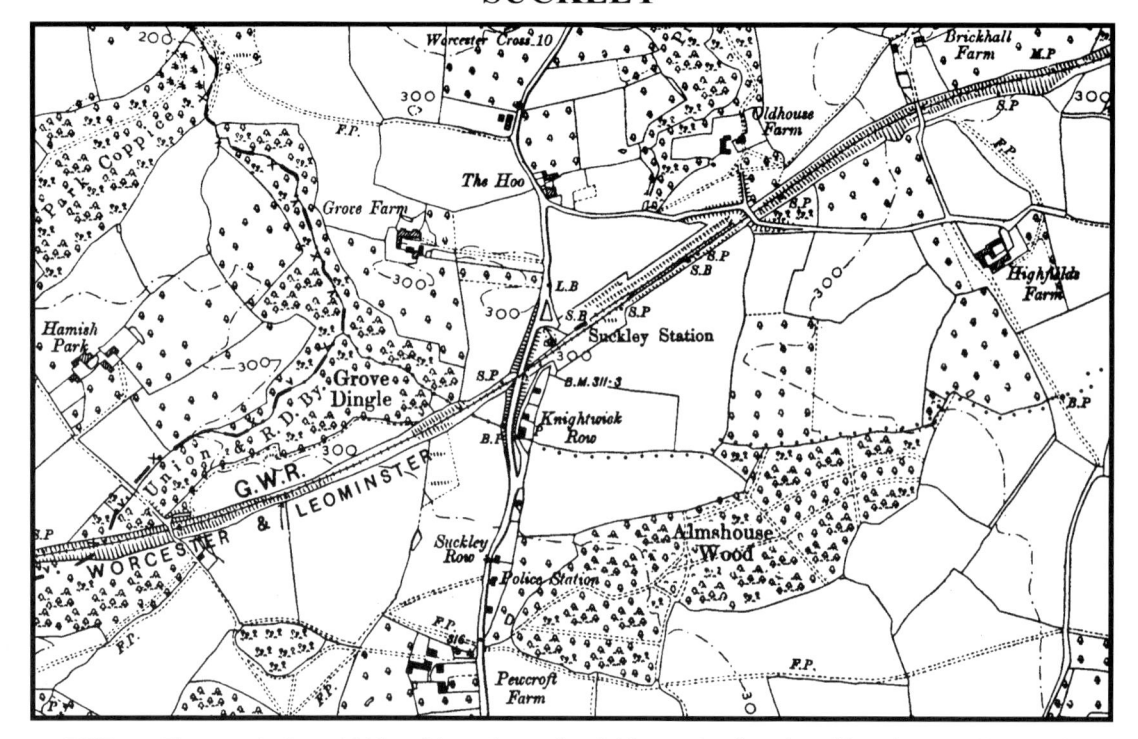

VIII.　　The map is from 1905 and is at the scale of 6 ins to 1 mile. The village is 1½ miles south of the station. The population at the turn of the century was 628.

22.　　We start our survey with three pictures from 1954, this one being taken from the road bridge. The Worcestershire/Herefordshire boundary is at the bridge in the background. The station opened nine months after the line, on 1st February 1878. (J.Moss/R.S.Carpenter)

23. This was the first of three passing places on the route. Cash was presumably limited when this location was reached, as a timber building was provided. An average of three staff members was employed between 1903 and 1938. (J.Moss/R.S.Carpenter)

24. A boarded crossing was provided here, unlike the one for the staff. Access to most rural goods yards was by trailing points. There was another connection beyond the wagon. Closure dates are as in caption 18. (J.Moss/R.S.Carpenter)

25.   The 5.50pm Worcester Shrub Hill to Bromyard was worked by 0-6-0PT no. 3725 on 17th July 1959. The loop, second platform and signal box came into use in April 1908, but all ceased to be used on 21st October 1956, hence the lack of signals in this view. The frame had 21 levers. (H.C.Casserley)

26.   All passengers are elderly in this 1962 record; others were taking to motor cars at this time. The GWR twin railcars were numbered 35 to 38 and had AEC engines with Swindon coachwork. (Stations UK)

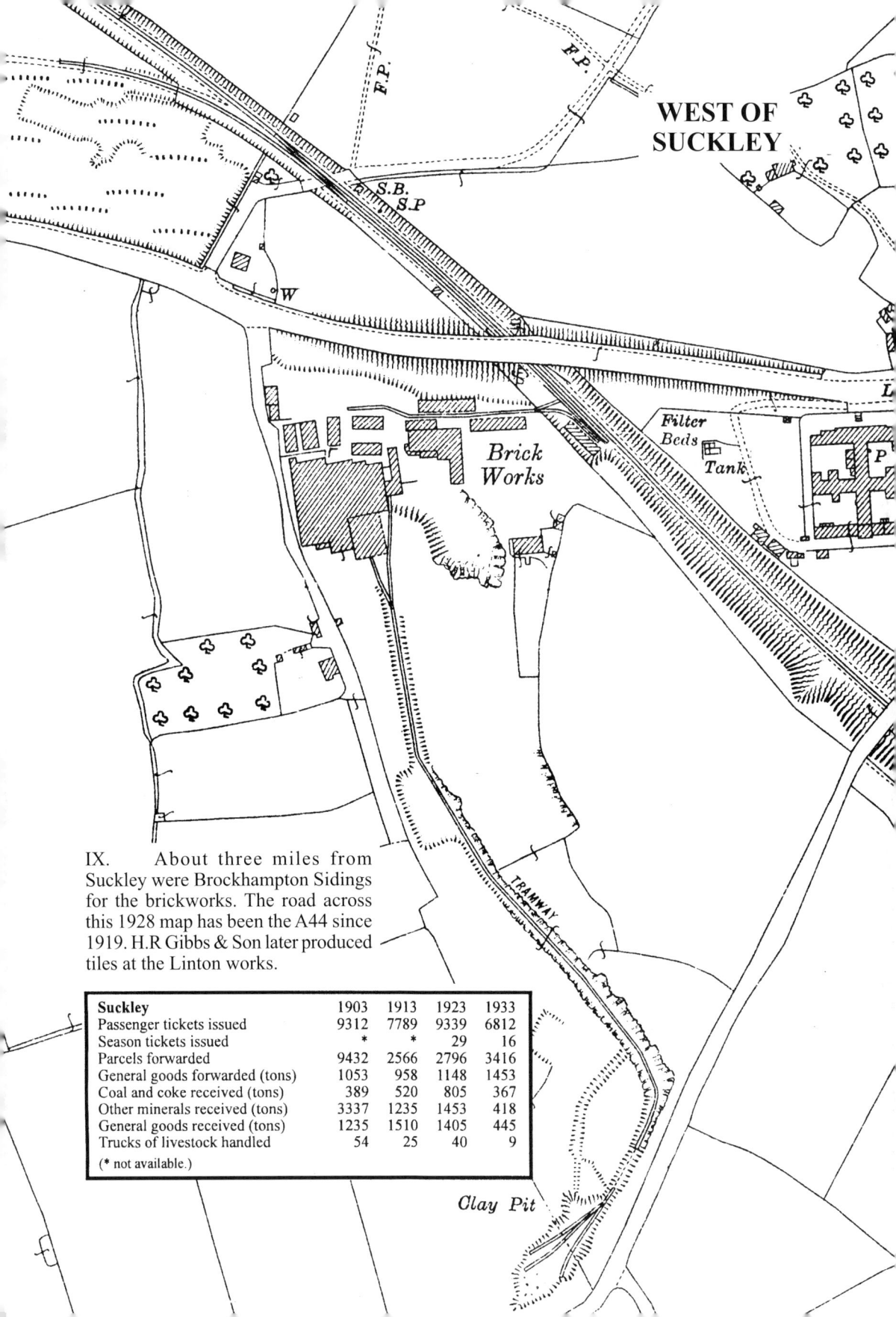

IX. About three miles from Suckley were Brockhampton Sidings for the brickworks. The road across this 1928 map has been the A44 since 1919. H.R Gibbs & Son later produced tiles at the Linton works.

Suckley	1903	1913	1923	1933
Passenger tickets issued	9312	7789	9339	6812
Season tickets issued	*	*	29	16
Parcels forwarded	9432	2566	2796	3416
General goods forwarded (tons)	1053	958	1148	1453
Coal and coke received (tons)	389	520	805	367
Other minerals received (tons)	3337	1235	1453	418
General goods received (tons)	1235	1510	1405	445
Trucks of livestock handled	54	25	40	9
(* not available.)				

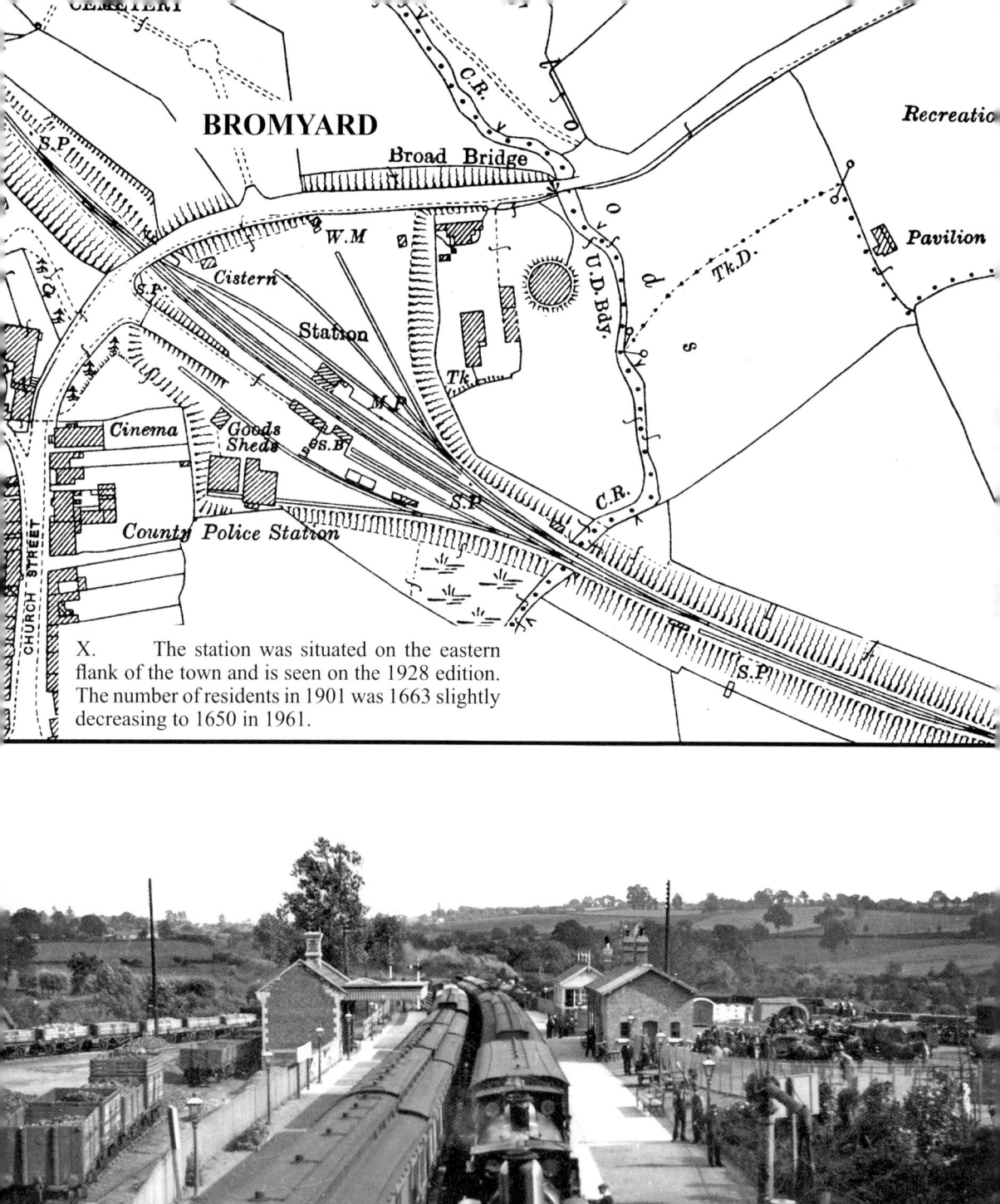

X. The station was situated on the eastern flank of the town and is seen on the 1928 edition. The number of residents in 1901 was 1663 slightly decreasing to 1650 in 1961.

(lower left) 27. This view towards Worcester is thought to be from the 1905-10 period and to feature trains for hop pickers. The number of employees at the station doubled between 1903 and 1938 rising from 7 to 14, which included staff at Rowden Mill and Steen's Bridge. (R.S.Carpenter coll.)

28. Nos. 2541 and 2551 are seen from a train arriving from Worcester on 11th September 1952, only days before services to Leominster ceased. (H.C.Casserley)

29. There had been a locomotive shed on the right of this picture until the route was extended westward in 1897. No. 4664 is running round on 5th June 1959. (R.M.Casserley)

30. Part of the down platform was converted to a garden in April 1955. The store on the left was then a recent addition for bagged fertiliser and feedstuff. (Stations UK)

31. A pair of ex-GWR railcars are seen in 1962. The signal box was in use from 1897 until 7th September 1964, when all traffic ceased. There were 29 levers. The two-foot gauge Bromyard & Linton Light Railway was established in the goods yard by Bob Palmer in 1968 and the line was later extended to terminate in the yard of Linton Tile Works, almost one mile distant. (Stations UK)

ROWDEN MILL

XI. The 1928 survey includes the formal title of the line and also the mill itself. The nearest village was Bredenbury, one mile to the west, which had a population of 119 in 1901.

32. The station had been designated a halt in the late 1940s. Very few staff were employed at the station between 1903 and 1931 falling from two to just one person. Seen soon after closure, the goods yard had ceased to handle traffic on 1st September 1949. Cattle and passengers were segregated on their approach to trains at this location. (J.Moss/R.S.Carpenter)

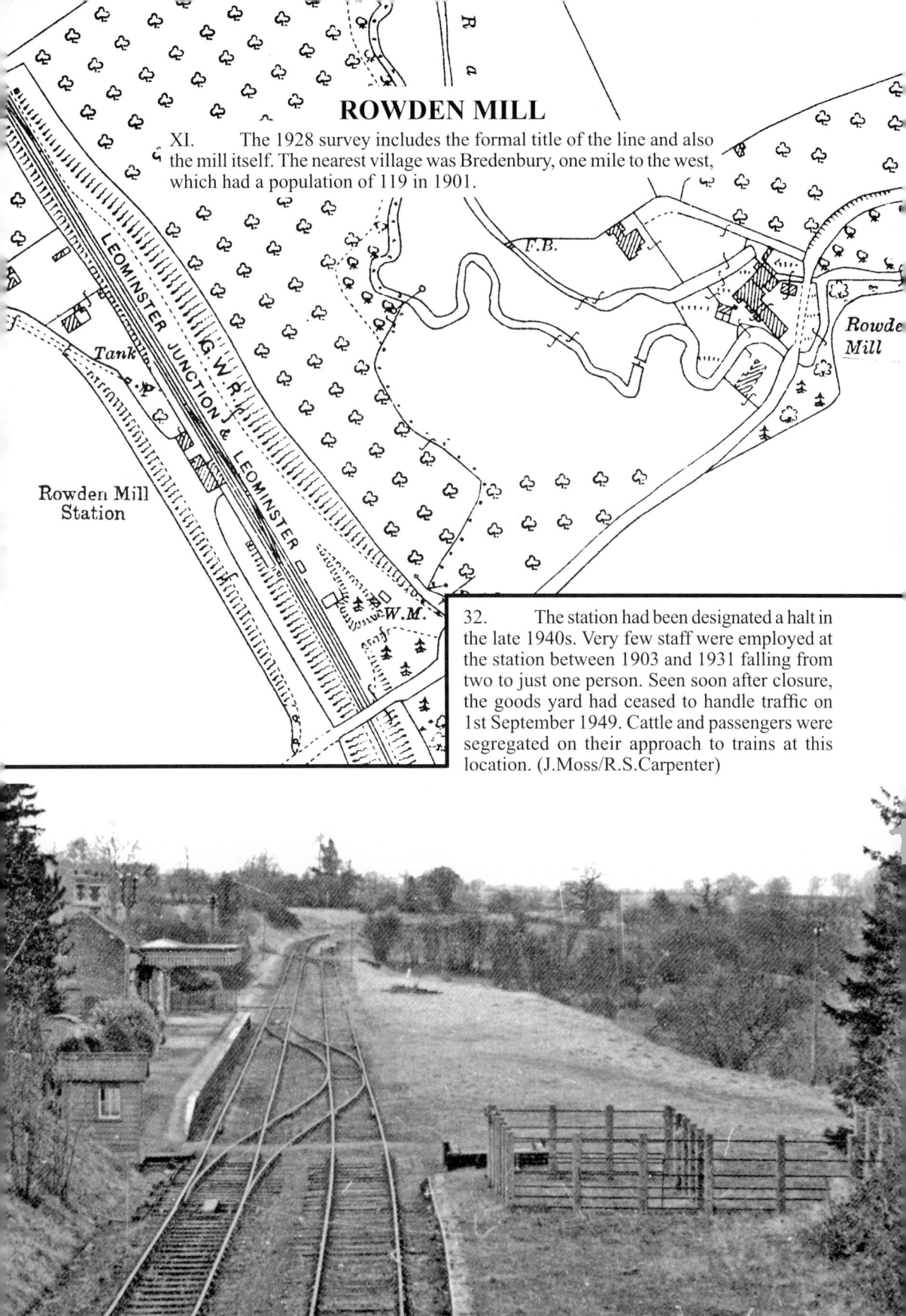

33. The station had been derelict for 30 years when purchased by John Wilkinson in 1984 and the platforms had largely vanished under trees. An astonishing restoration programme ensued and the former Taunton District inspection saloon arrived in 1992 and is seen in 2004, along with one of five trolleys. There was also a class 03 diesel, a fruit van and a brake van. The premises are not open to the public. They received a Railway Heritage Award in 1992. (J.Wilkinson)

Rowden Mill	1903	1913	1923	1933
Passenger tickets issued	5600	3792	4457	2109
Season tickets issued	*	*	25	3
Parcels forwarded	3399	3099	1908	522
General goods forwarded (tons)	148	279	238	159
Coal and coke received (tons)	224	273	89	18
Other minerals received (tons)	835	427	616	316
General goods received (tons)	650	622	582	70
Trucks of livestock handled	2	8	31	2

(* not available.)

FENCOTE

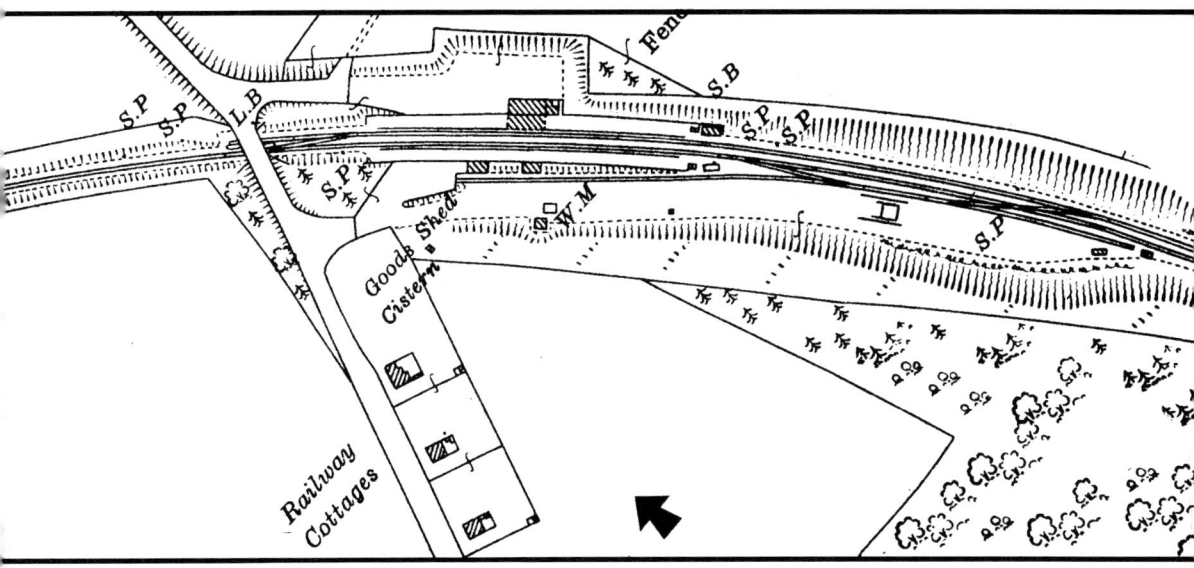

XII. The station was situated on a lane north of the hamlet of Bilfield and was named after a nearby abbey. The 1928 map confirms that it was a thinly populated area. However, this was a convenient place for a passing loop.

34. The main building was recorded from a train from Worcester on 11th September 1952. The box had 23 levers. The station had an average of three staff between 1903 and 1931. (H.C.Casserley)

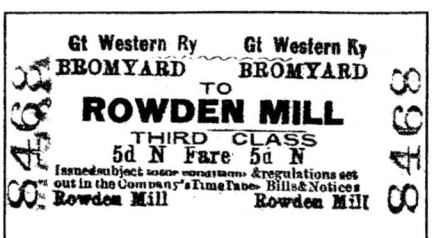

35. Although totally closed in 1952, the track remained in place until 1959. Thus the Stephenson Locomotive Society was able to operate a special train over the route on 26th April 1958. The train was hauled by 2-6-2T no. 4571. The goods shed is on the left. (R.M.Casserley)

36. The station was intact when purchased by ex-Leominster signalman Ken Matthews in 1980. Seen 20 years later, the premises were in impeccable condition with an inspection saloon standing in the platform. Beyond it is the perfectly restored signal box, which had been fitted with a lever frame from Gerrards Cross, cut down from 33 to 23 levers. The coach had been used for camping purposes at Dawlish Warren for many years and was ex-LMS. The site is strictly private, but can be glimpsed from the road. An occasional open day is held here and at Rowden Mill. (K.Matthews)

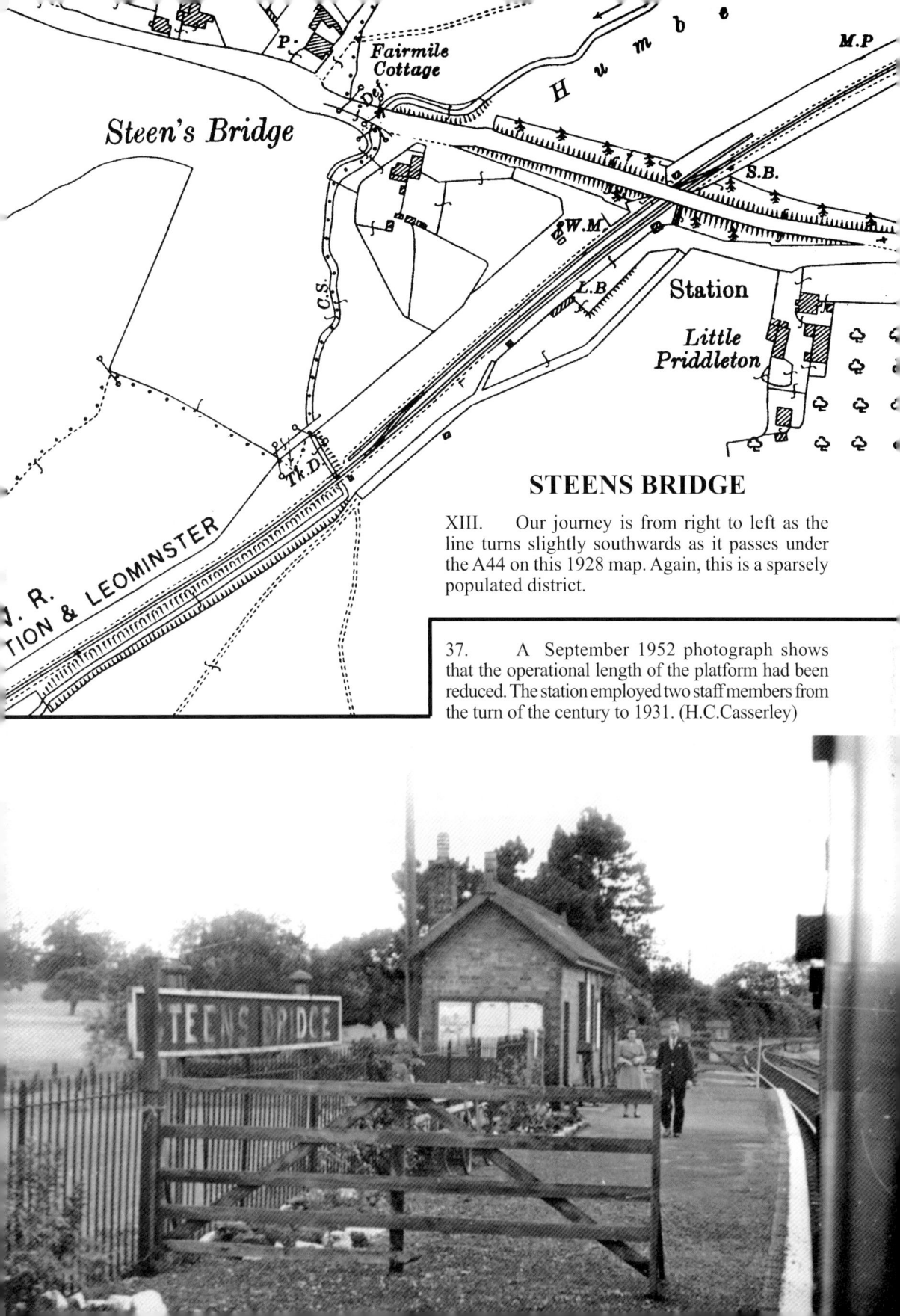

STEENS BRIDGE

XIII. Our journey is from right to left as the line turns slightly southwards as it passes under the A44 on this 1928 map. Again, this is a sparsely populated district.

37. A September 1952 photograph shows that the operational length of the platform had been reduced. The station employed two staff members from the turn of the century to 1931. (H.C.Casserley)

38. The extent of the loop was recorded in 1954. It would have been much used when the station was a terminus in 1884-97. (Stations UK)

Steens Bridge	1903	1913	1923	1933
Passenger tickets issued	4630	4508	5160	2356
Season tickets issued	*	*	2	18
Parcels forwarded	915	1616	1316	1823
General goods forwarded (tons)	83	342	190	43
Coal and coke received (tons)	252	453	202	128
Other minerals received (tons)	534	1632	710	1024
General goods received (tons)	242	308	290	49
Trucks of livestock handled	2	-	3	14

(* not available.)

STOKE PRIOR HALT

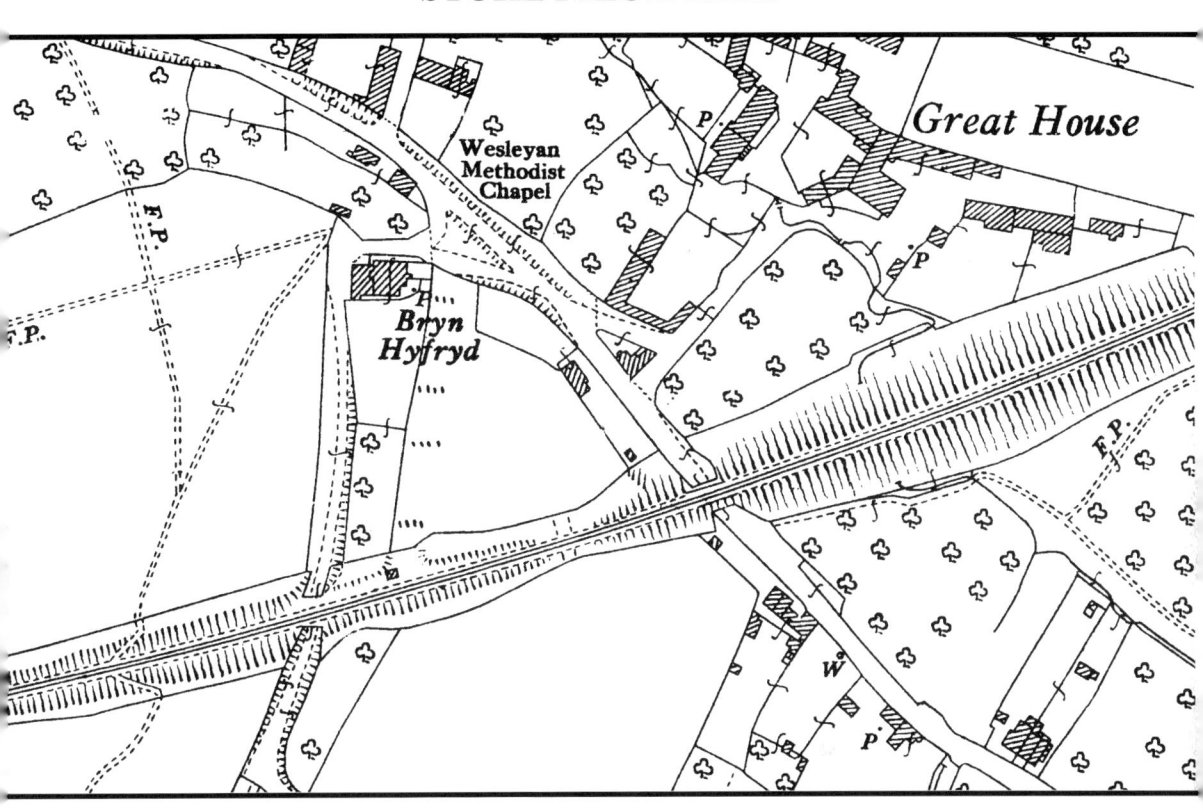

XIV. The halt opened on 8th July 1929 and thus does not appear on this 1928 edition. It was close to the bridge, right of centre, on the north side of the line. The village had a population of 355 in 1901.

39. Facilities were minimal. The oil lamp was the responsibility of the guard who was supposed to remove it during daylight hours and after the last train. The mileage of 145½ is from Paddington. (H.C.Casserley)

LEOMINSTER

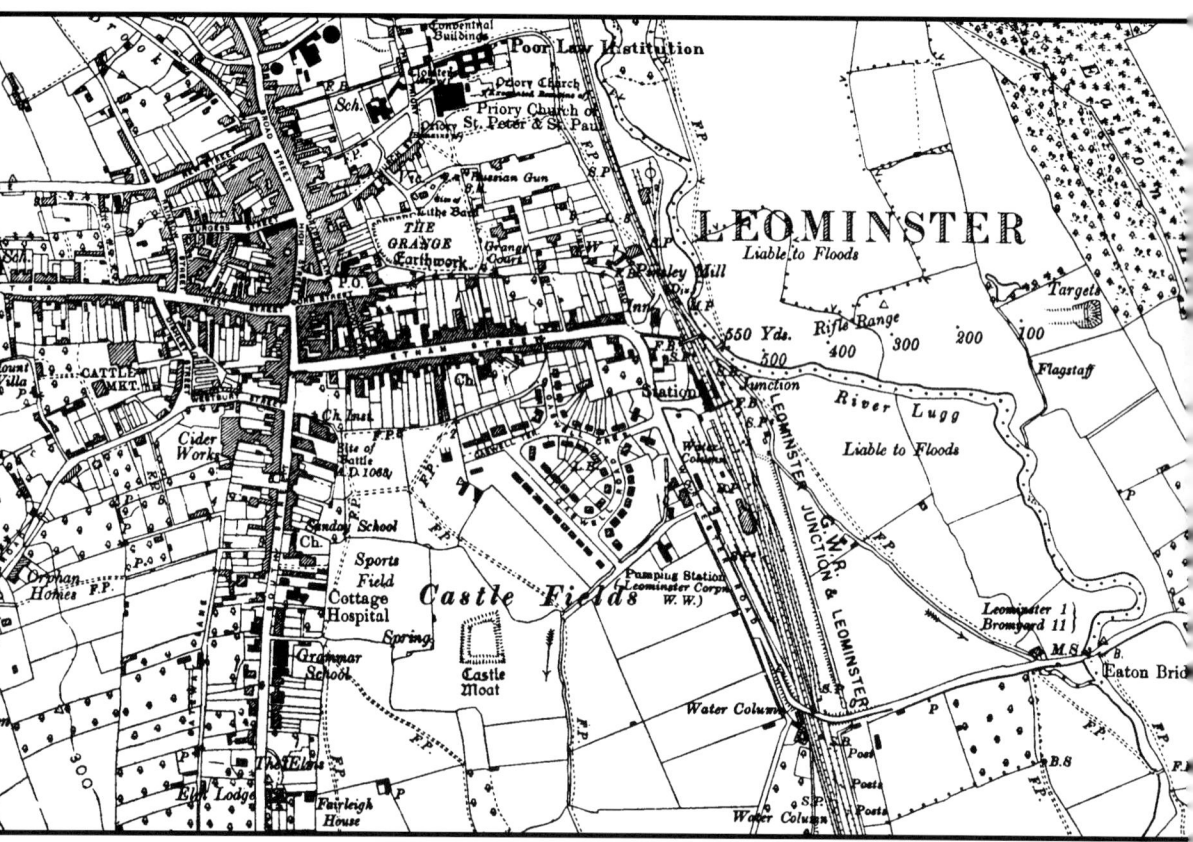

(left) XV. The 1930 edition at 6 ins to 1 mile shows the close proximity of the station to the town centre. The town was populated by 5826 people in 1901 which rose to 6530 by 1961.

(lower left) 40. This southward panorama is from a postcard of about 1905. The five platforms gave generous provision for allowing fast trains to pass slow ones on the Shrewsbury-Hereford route and to terminate trains from Worcester, New Radnor and Presteigne. There were as many as 20 per day in the 1930s. (R.S.Carpenter coll.)

41. Trains on the Kington branch used the station between 1857 and 1964. This may be one, photographed in 1952. The elevated signal box was in use from 1902 until 1964 and had 99 levers. (H.C.Casserley)

42. A northward view in 1954 has the engine shed in the distance; it was closed in 1962. The goods shed is behind the camera; freight traffic ceased on 2nd January 1967. (Stations UK)

3. Bransford Road to Ledbury

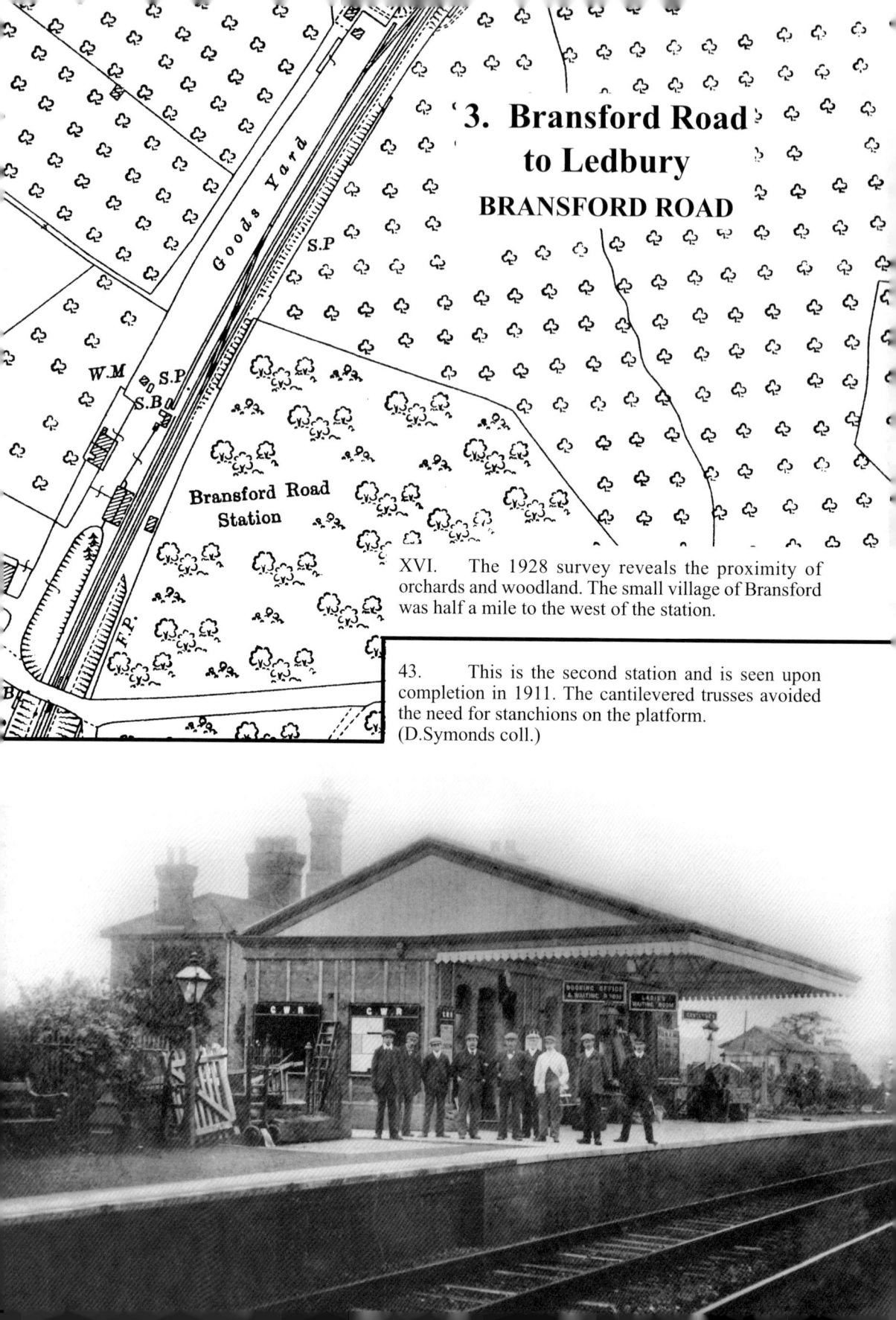

BRANSFORD ROAD

XVI. The 1928 survey reveals the proximity of orchards and woodland. The small village of Bransford was half a mile to the west of the station.

43. This is the second station and is seen upon completion in 1911. The cantilevered trusses avoided the need for stanchions on the platform. (D.Symonds coll.)

44. A view towards Malvern shows some of the trusses and the bridge which carries the lane from Powick. There was a signal box here until 1956. (D.Symonds coll.)

45. A northward panorama in the 1930s contains a scene that changed little over the next thirty years. The signal box and goods yard closed in February 1964, staffing ceased in November of that year and the station closed on 5th April 1965. Only the house remains. (Lens of Sutton coll.)

NEWLAND HALT

46. The halt opened on 18th March 1929 and closed on 5th April 1965. The signal box was called Stocks Lane until 18th June 1943, when it became Newland East when a loop and seven sidings came into use for military purposes. (Stations UK)

47. Newland East box had 33 levers and was still in use when photographed in 2003. The seven sidings were used for track pre-assembly from 1954 until 1964. The site was subsequently occupied by caravans. (V.Mitchell)

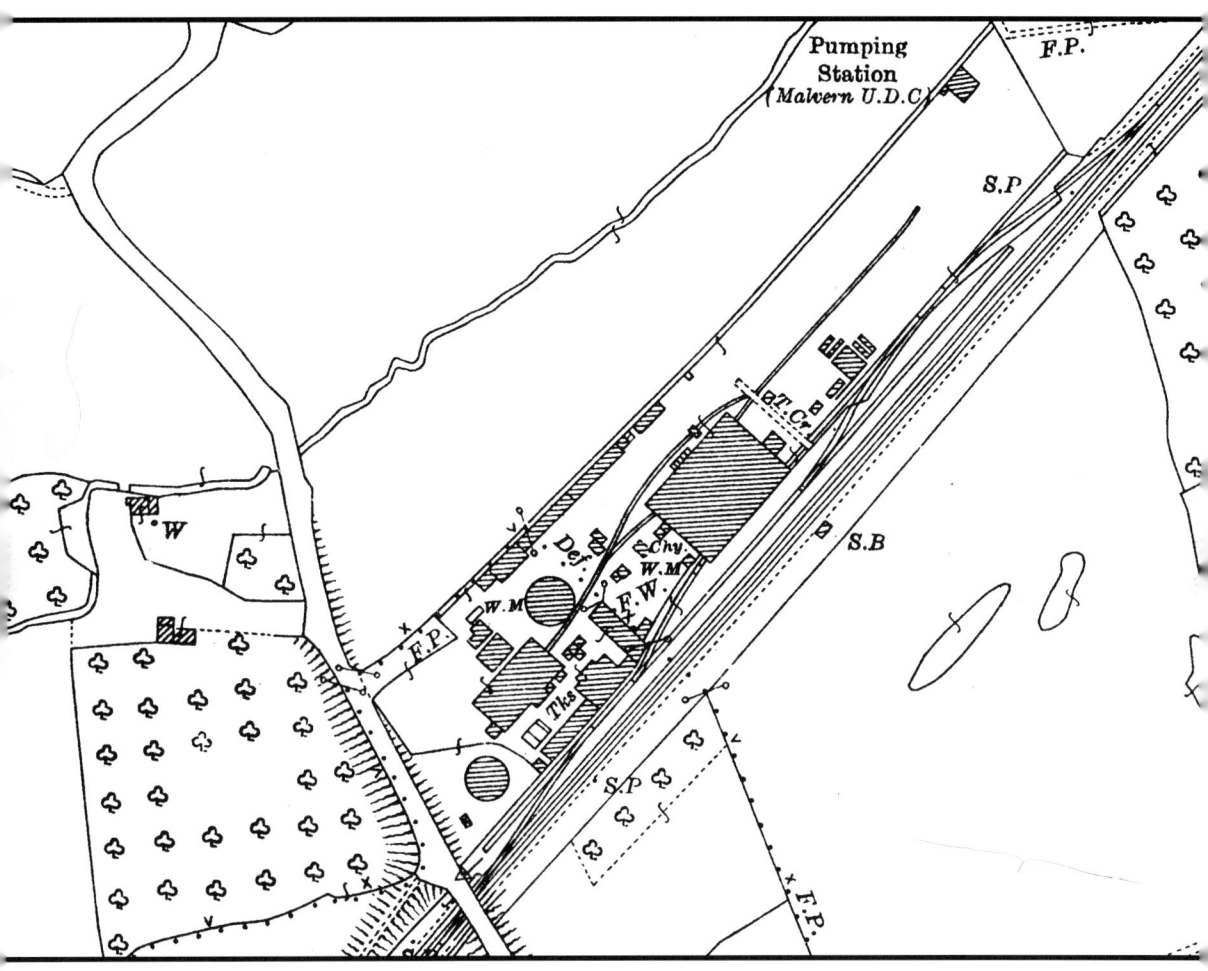

XVII. The 1927 map includes the gasworks and a signal box which became Newland West in 1943 to control the south end of the new loop. The works and box closed in 1964.

Malvern Link	1903	1913	1923	1933
Passenger tickets issued	115671	104121	128519	85850
Season tickets issued	*	*	941	3743
Parcels forwarded	25328	31837	35525	9313
General goods forwarded (tons)	2906	3314	3245	2505
Coal and coke received (tons)	14694	13679	8467	3668
Other minerals received (tons)	6071	4570	3313	1381
General goods received (tons)	11245	10541	10922	8456
Trucks of livestock handled	234	222	110	48
(* not available.)				

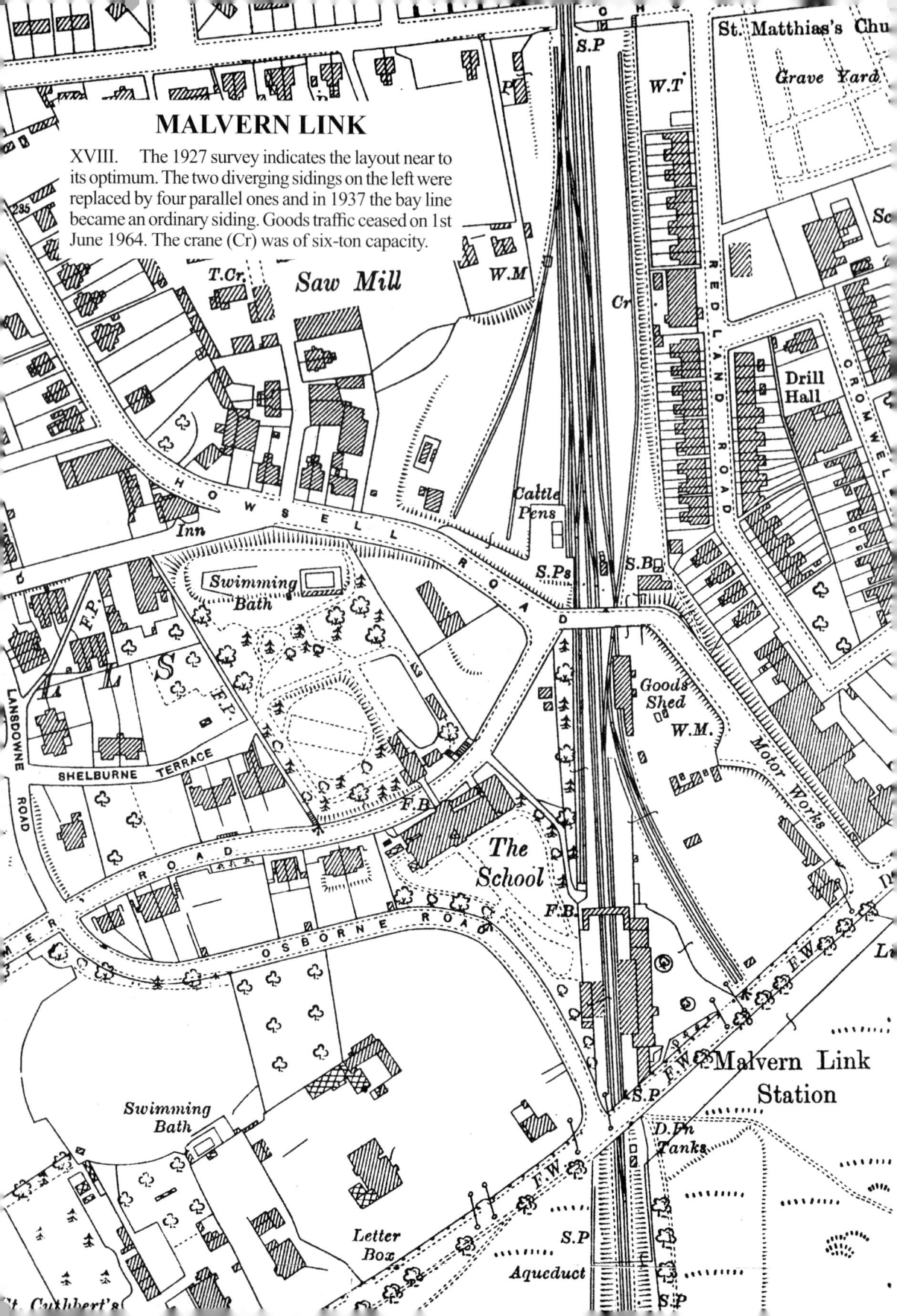

MALVERN LINK

XVIII. The 1927 survey indicates the layout near to its optimum. The two diverging sidings on the left were replaced by four parallel ones and in 1937 the bay line became an ordinary siding. Goods traffic ceased on 1st June 1964. The crane (Cr) was of six-ton capacity.

48. The architectural details are worthy of close study at this important location. Two bridges obscure the 42-lever signal box, which closed on 21st December 1965 and is marked S.B. on the map. The number of staff at the station gradually decreased between 1903 and 1938 from 24 to just 14. (D.Symonds coll.)

49. Another view northwards and this includes the roof of the up waiting room. All the fine structures were cleared away, leaving unprotected platforms. The footbridge span was retained, but new steps made. (Stations UK)

50. Small cedar-clad buildings were erected on both sides. This is the up side where a ticket office was still staffed on weekday mornings when this Thames Turbo was recorded in 2003. (V.Mitchell)

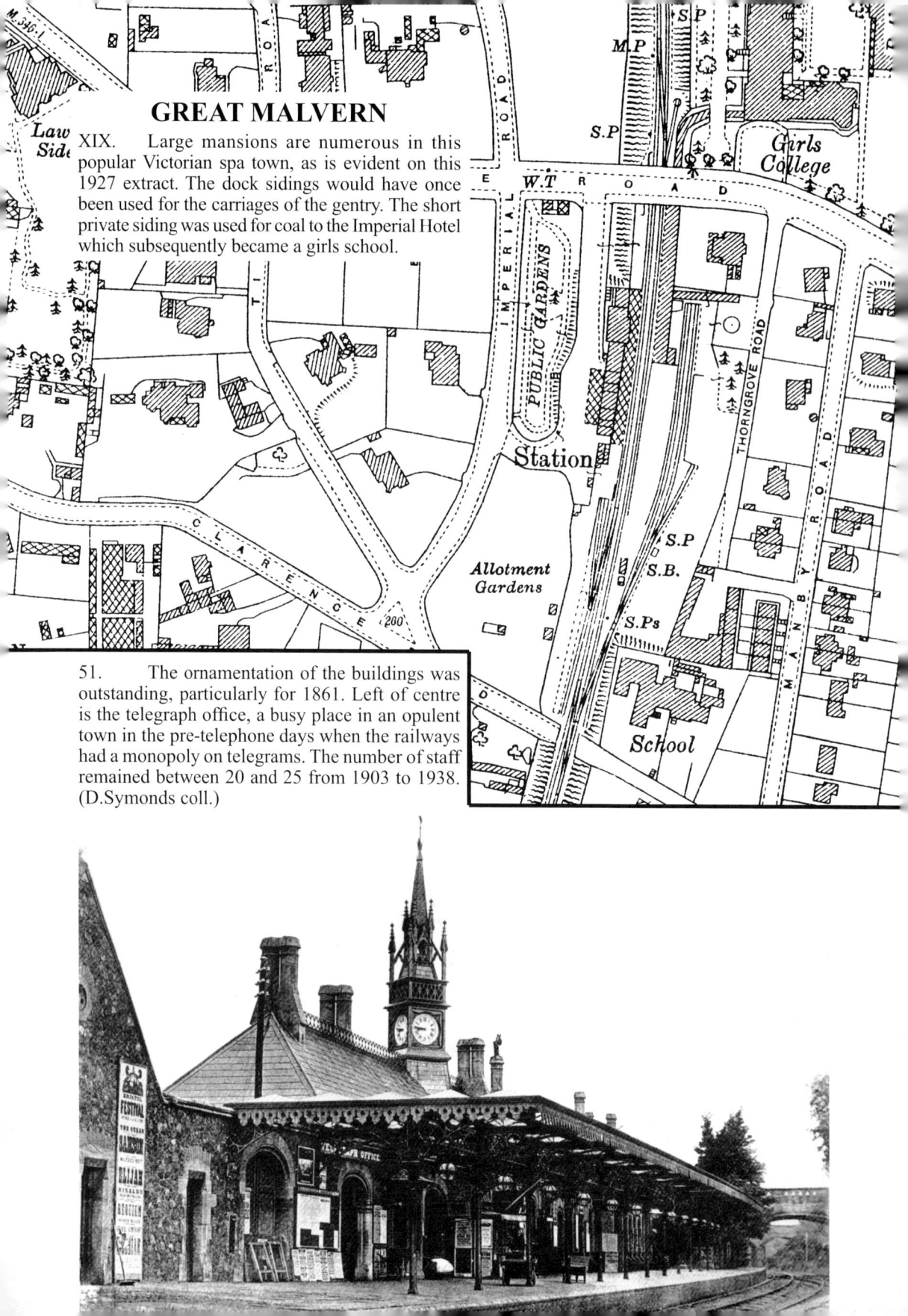

GREAT MALVERN

XIX. Large mansions are numerous in this popular Victorian spa town, as is evident on this 1927 extract. The dock sidings would have once been used for the carriages of the gentry. The short private siding was used for coal to the Imperial Hotel which subsequently became a girls school.

51. The ornamentation of the buildings was outstanding, particularly for 1861. Left of centre is the telegraph office, a busy place in an opulent town in the pre-telephone days when the railways had a monopoly on telegrams. The number of staff remained between 20 and 25 from 1903 to 1938. (D.Symonds coll.)

52.	No. 722 was a 4-4-0 of the 717 class and is recorded as having been photographed at the down platform in the late 1890s. (P.Q.Treloar coll.)

53.	A photograph from the same location on 9th September 1949 includes ex-LMS class 2P 2-6-2T no. 40116 standing with a single coach train for Ashchurch. Five such trains terminated here on weekdays at that period. (H.C.Casserley)

54. The up dock lines are evident as 2-6-2T no. 4567 departs west with an autocoach in 1951. The signal box had 36 levers and functioned until 14th March 1965, when all the sidings were taken out of use. (T.Hancock coll.)

55. The splendid clock tower had been destroyed by the time that this photo was taken in July 1965. The ornate canopy had also gone. The building was listed in 1970 and was thus spared further desecration. (Lens of Sutton)

56. This is the 13.36 *from* Birmingham to Hereford on 26th April 1982. Lack of cooperation by drivers resulted in the destination panels being painted over. (T.Heavyside)

57. The 15.40 "Thames Express" service from Great Malvern to Paddington is about to depart on 31st July 1993. Set 166207 (Network South East) is on a joint Regional Railways/NSE working. (N.W.Sprinks)

58. The buffet and station features were renovated to high standards, the floral motifs at the top of each column being painted colourfully. Seen on 25th July 1995 is the 14.27 Great Malvern to Hednesford in Staffordshire. (N.W.Sprinks)

NORTH OF MALVERN WELLS

59.   A down goods loop was added in April 1901 and is on the left of this view of a Cardiff to Birmingham express in the 1940s. The station is beyond the bridge and the loco is no. 5977 *Beckford Hall*. (J.Scott Morgan coll./R.S.Carpenter)

60.   The entire loop is seen from the bridge on 26th April 1982, as a DMU slows down prior to reversal over the crossover behind the camera and under the bridge. (T.Heavyside)

XX. The 1905 survey at 6 ins to 1 mile has the GWR station lower left. To the right of it is the MR double track, that company's station being beyond the lower border of the map.

61. A postcard view from around 1910 includes the crossover and down goods loop. Throughout the 1930s the staffing levels averaged about seven men. (Lens of Sutton coll.)

62. Four or five local trains from Worcester terminated here daily in 1946, such as this 1400 class 0-4-2T with two autocoaches. It will reverse under the bridge and allow the waiting goods train to proceed. (J.Scott Morgan coll./R.S.Carpenter)

63. Railcar no. 7 is seen from the down platform probably on the same day. It may have reversed on the crossover beyond the signal box, which is seen again in the next picture. The goods yard closed on 1st June 1964 and the station followed on 5th April 1965.
(J.Scott Morgan coll./R.S.Carpenter)

64. One goods siding (left) was retained by the engineers. The crossover under the bridge and the loop beyond it were used by terminating trains. The 40-lever signal box was photographed in March 2003. The single line to Ledbury commences behind the camera. (V.Mitchell)

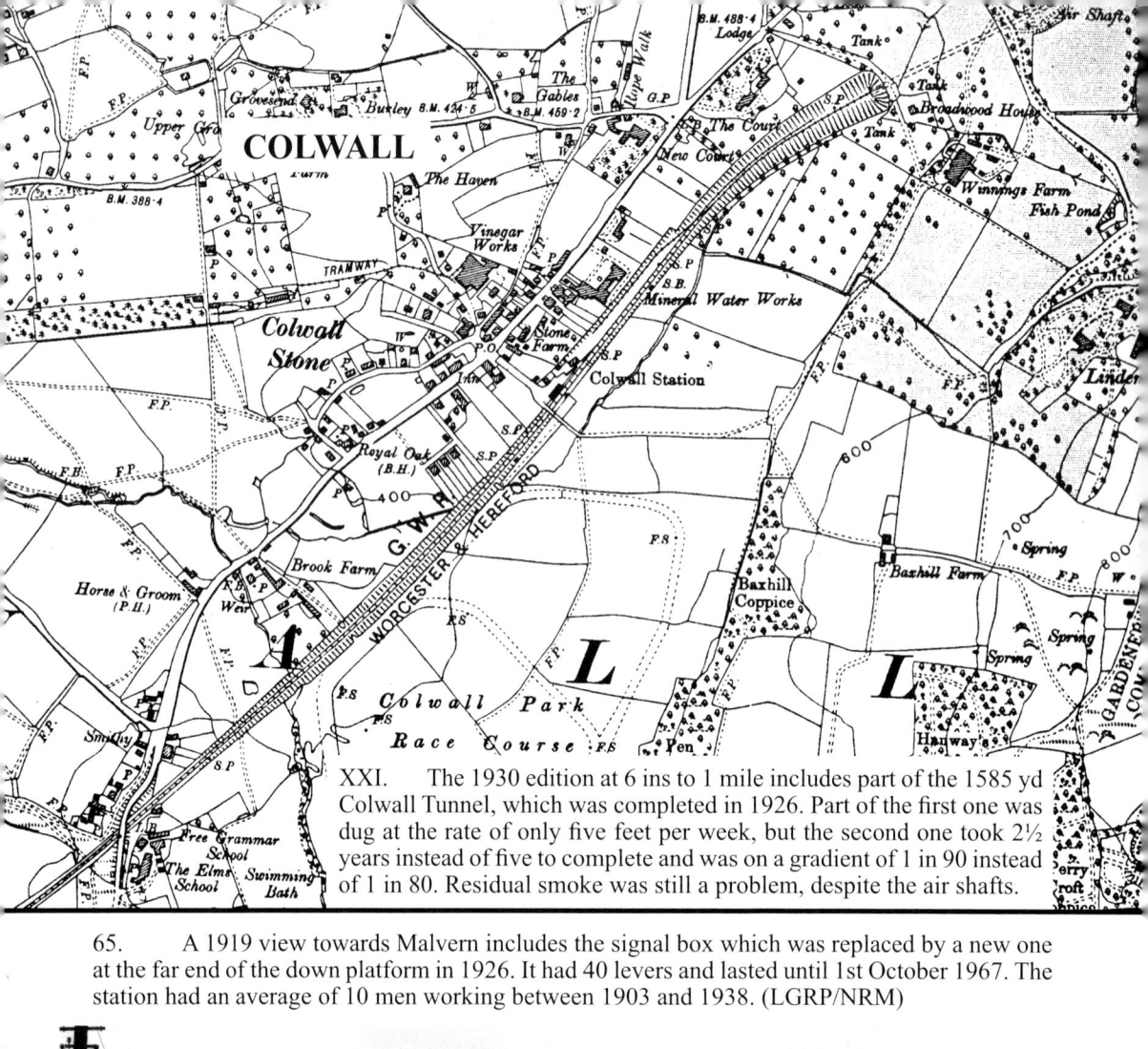

XXI.   The 1930 edition at 6 ins to 1 mile includes part of the 1585 yd Colwall Tunnel, which was completed in 1926. Part of the first one was dug at the rate of only five feet per week, but the second one took 2½ years instead of five to complete and was on a gradient of 1 in 90 instead of 1 in 80. Residual smoke was still a problem, despite the air shafts.

65.   A 1919 view towards Malvern includes the signal box which was replaced by a new one at the far end of the down platform in 1926. It had 40 levers and lasted until 1st October 1967. The station had an average of 10 men working between 1903 and 1938. (LGRP/NRM)

66. The line was singled between Colwall and Ledbury tunnels on 1st October 1967, the goods yard having closed on 2nd November 1964 leaving the goods shed in isolation, as seen on 26th April 1982. The train is the 09.15 *from* Oxford to Hereford. (T.Heavyside)

67. The bridge was retained for the benefit of footpath users and a departure indicator was added nearby. This 2003 view includes the garden maintained by local residents in memory of the last station master. (V.Mitchell)

68. No. 47509 *Albion* approaches with the 17.00 Paddington to Hereford service in April 1982. The train is curved vertically as it passes over the summit. The population rose to 2045 in 1961 from 1892 at the turn of the century. (T.Heavyside)

EAST OF LEDBURY

69.   The 1323 yd-long Ledbury Tunnel was built to small dimensions, like the first Colwall Tunnel. Neither tunnel had tokens, but had lock-and-block instruments in the boxes. The nearest was behind the camera until the singling. It was called Ledbury North End and had 16 levers. Further north was the 15-lever Cummings Crossing box, which lasted until April 1954. No. 50040 *Leviathan* is hauling the 18.50 Hereford to Paddington on 26th April 1982. (T.Heavyside)

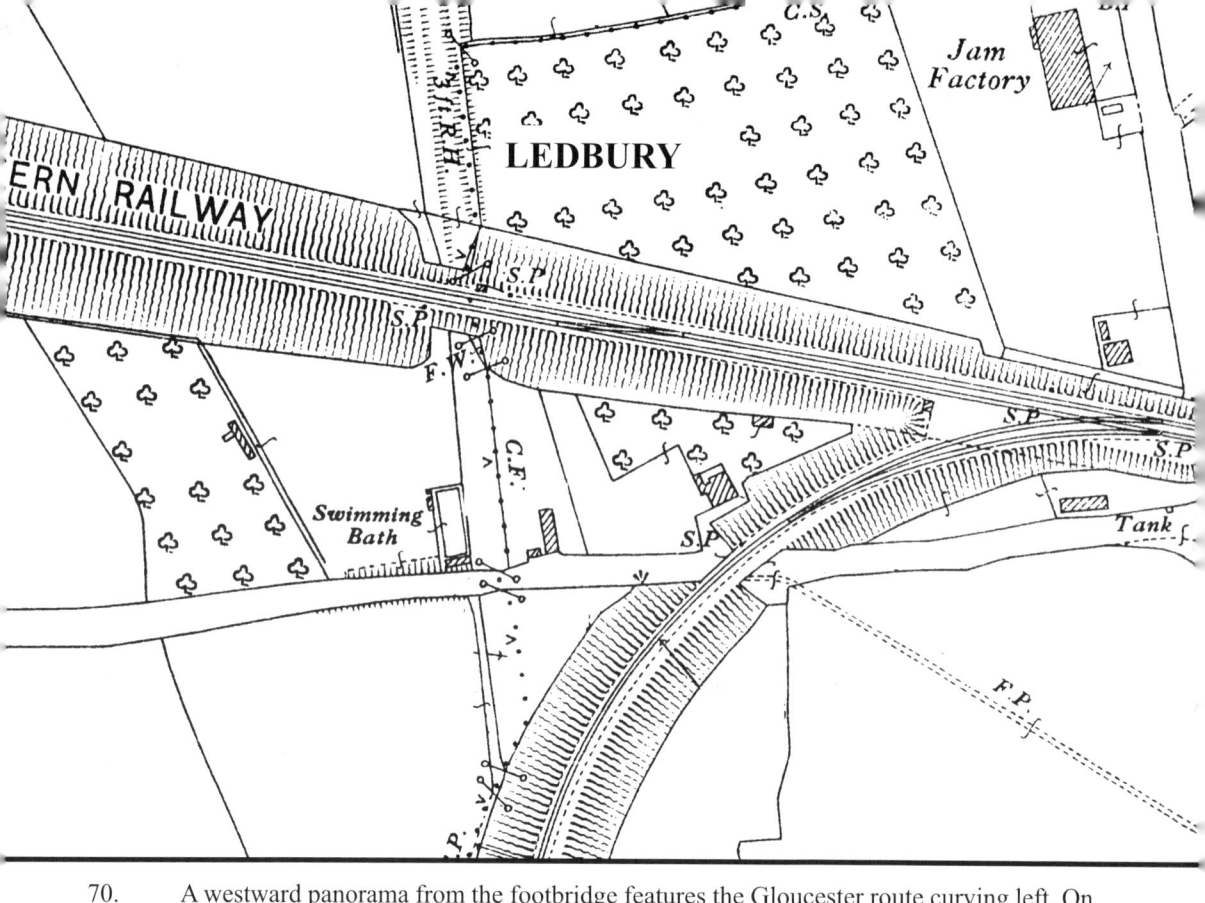

70.   A westward panorama from the footbridge features the Gloucester route curving left. On it was Ledbury Branch box until 1925; it had only six levers. The staff levels ranged from between 21 to 29 people from 1903 to 1938. (D.Symonds coll.)

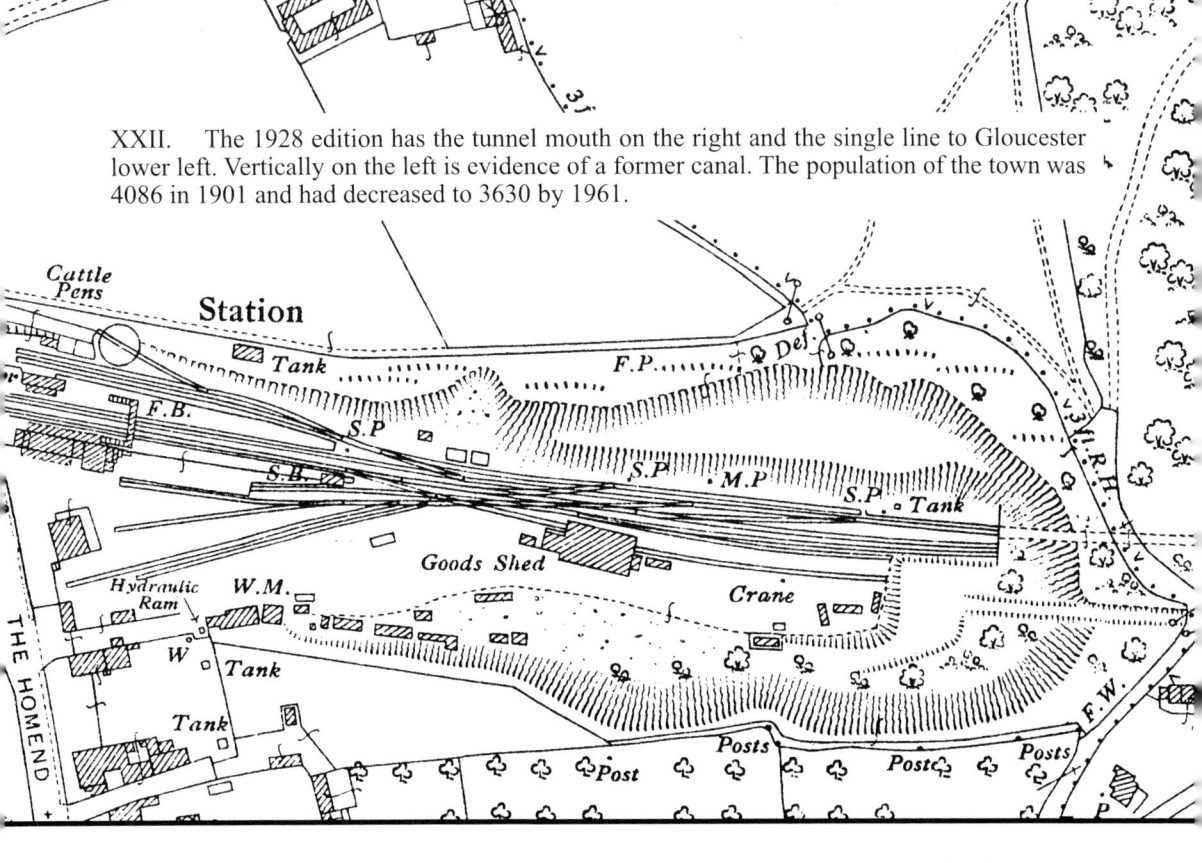

XXII. The 1928 edition has the tunnel mouth on the right and the single line to Gloucester lower left. Vertically on the left is evidence of a former canal. The population of the town was 4086 in 1901 and had decreased to 3630 by 1961.

71. It is almost one mile to the town centre and so many used a bus if available. This one was recorded in 1949. The station was named "Ledbury Junction" from 1885 to 1959. (Lens of Sutton coll.)

72.   Railway observers witness the arrival of 0-4-2T no. 1401 with an autocoach from Gloucester in the early 1950s. The hole in the footbridge enabled the signalman to check the starting signals. (Lens of Sutton coll.)

73.   The coal stage, turntable and cattle dock could all be seen from the up platform. This scene was recorded in June 1951. A banking engine was often to be seen here or beside the goods shed, waiting to help trains through Ledbury Tunnel. (D.B.Clayton)

74. An ex-GWR railcar has an ordinary coach in tow as it emerges from the tunnel on 27th September 1952. These cars were introduced on to Oxford-Hereford services in 1938. The goods yard closed on 1st November 1965. The crane power at the station was 6 tons. (A.J.Pike/F.Hornby coll.)

75. The starting signal is obscured by the water column as a railcar waits to depart for Gloucester on 27th June 1959, only weeks before the service was withdrawn. (Lens of Sutton coll.)

76. A 1964 view shows grass where the branch lines had been, but the buildings were still intact and included a "General Waiting Room". The Leadon Valley is in the middle distance. The double connection to the branch had been reduced to one from the down line in 1957. The line ahead to Shelwick Junction was singled between 20th October and 11th November 1984. (M.A.N.Johnston)

77. A Worcester to Hereford DMU arrives on 26th April 1982, having just passed the siding on which Gloucester trains stood during their layover. Three sidings were retained by the engineers. (T.Heavyside)

78. One siding, a set of semaphore signals and a hole in the footbridge remained to be photographed on 26th March 2003. Staffing ceased on 28th October 1968, but local enterprise soon resulted in this garden shed being erected to house a ticket agency, which was open in the mornings. (V.Mitchell)

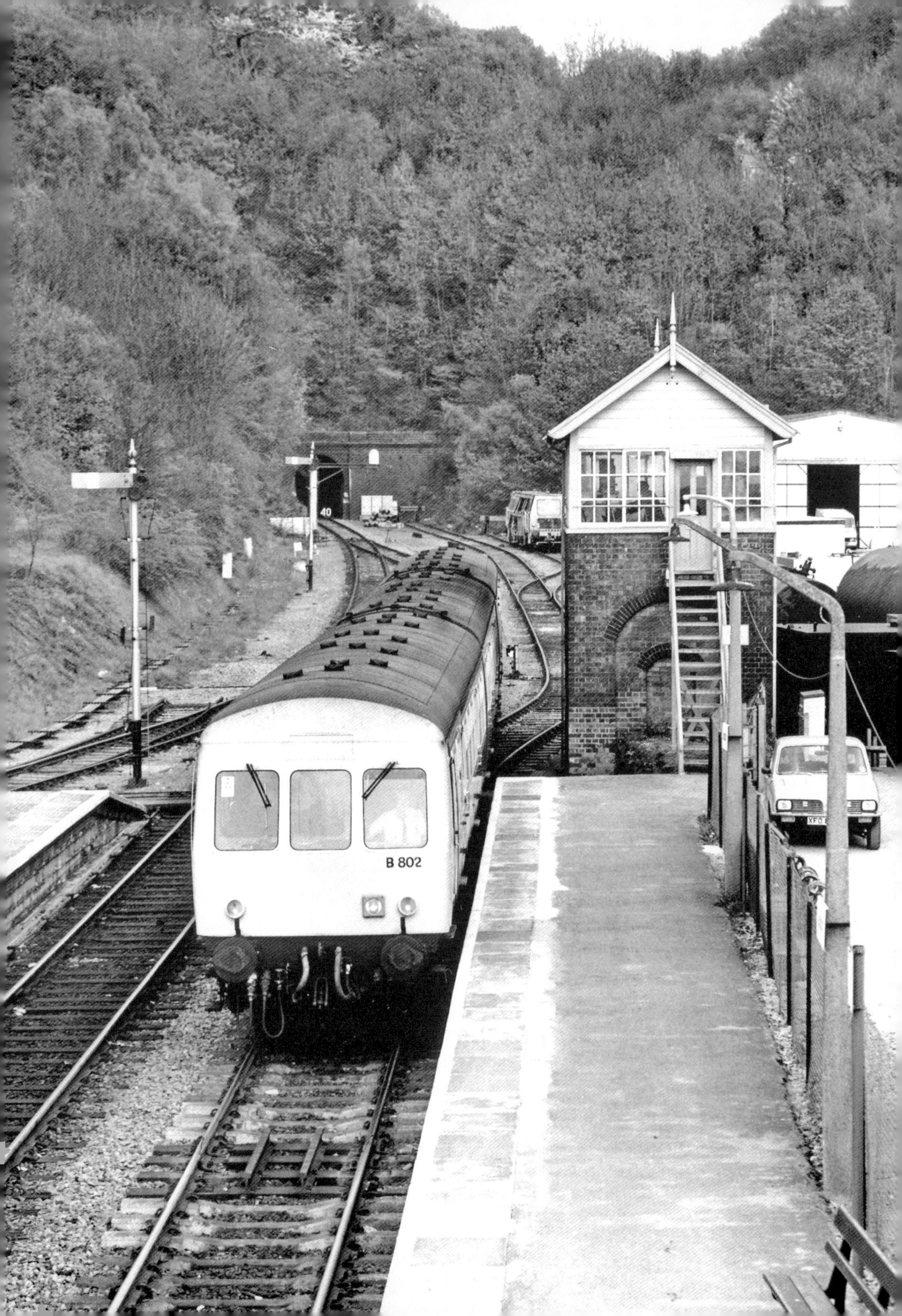
40
B 802

WEST OF LEDBURY

79. Ledbury Viaduct is 372 yds in length and passes over the River Leadon. The 17.00 Birmingham to Hereford DMU was recorded on 26th April 1982. (T.Heavyside)

Ledbury	1903	1913	1923	1933
Passenger tickets issued	52053	50355	50972	23404
Season tickets issued	*	*	262	201
Parcels forwarded	28779	39490	45857	30402
General goods forwarded (tons)	3638	3673	4704	2208
Coal and coke received (tons)	2421	3256	3616	2551
Other minerals received (tons)	4004	8563	4490	1355
General goods received (tons)	7905	9564	7426	5492
Trucks of livestock handled	487	579	620	306

(* not available.)

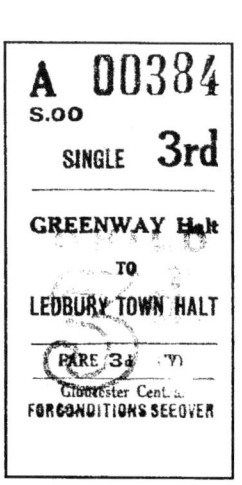

4. Ledbury to Gloucester
LEDBURY TOWN HALT

80.   The platform was within a few minutes walk of the centre of the town and was well used, particularly if there was a good connection at the main station. Part of the route northward is now a public footpath. (E.Wilmshurst)

81.   The halt opened belatedly on 26th November 1928 and minimal facilities were provided. At least there was an electric light. There was double track to Dymock until 4th January 1917, when the material was needed for World War I. There was a small ticket office at one period; 1809 tickets were issued from it in 1930. (R.S.Carpenter)

GREENWAY HALT

82. This came into use on 1st April 1937 and was three miles from Ledbury. Owners of perambulators were restricted in their mobility, as they were not accepted on buses. (E.Wilmshurst)

83. A northward view in 1959 shows that the pole route was on the alignment of the second track under the bridge. As at Ledbury Town, the platform had a loose cinder surface. (P.J.Garland/R.S.Carpenter)

DYMOCK

84. This is a view towards Ledbury in 1919. Cider and daffodils were notable goods despatched from here. The population of the town was 1316 at the turn of the century which had slightly decreased by 1961 to 1212. (LGRP/NRM)

XXIII. The station was close to the village centre. There is more evidence of the former canal on the left of this 1922 map.

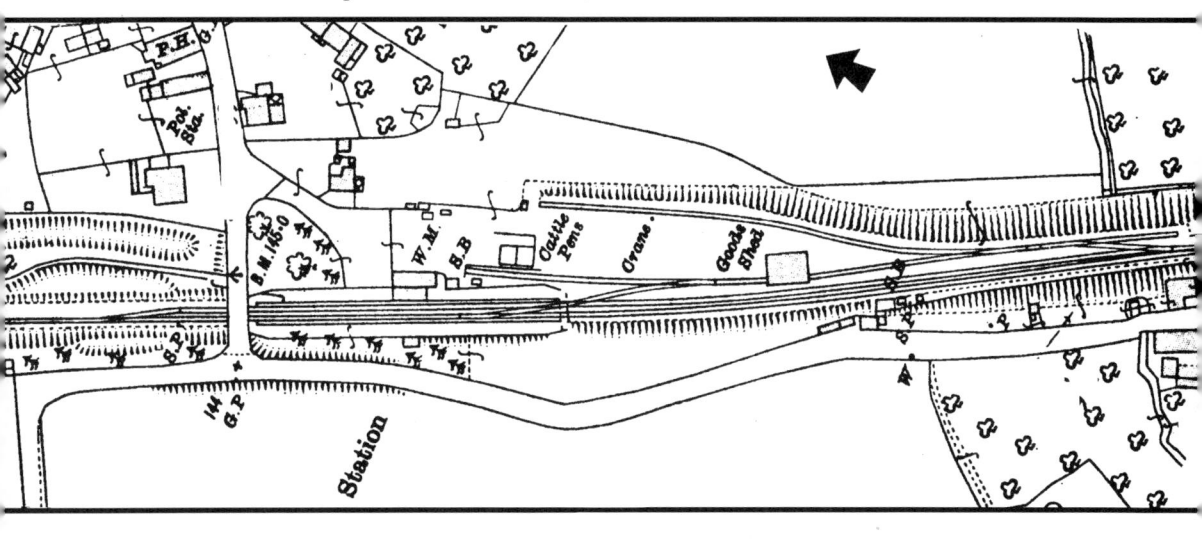

85. We can now enjoy two peaceful views recorded not long before closure to passengers in 1959. Admire the well kept gardens in this southward panorama. The station had a crane capable of lifting up to 5 tons. (R.S.Carpenter)

86. Goods service continued here until 1st June 1964, but the 16-lever signal box was down graded to a ground frame in 1959. The line northwards was lifted in 1960-62. On the left is a privately owned store for cattle feeds. (J.Moss/R.S.Carpenter coll.)

FOUR OAKS HALT

87. This halt opened on 16th October 1937 on a site slightly over two miles from Dymock. This peaceful spot is now close to the noisy M50. Another oil lamp hoist is included. (P.J.Garland/R.S.Carpenter coll.)

88. Shoppers destined for Ledbury join railcar W19W on 4th April 1959. The guard issued the tickets. (E.Wilmshurst)

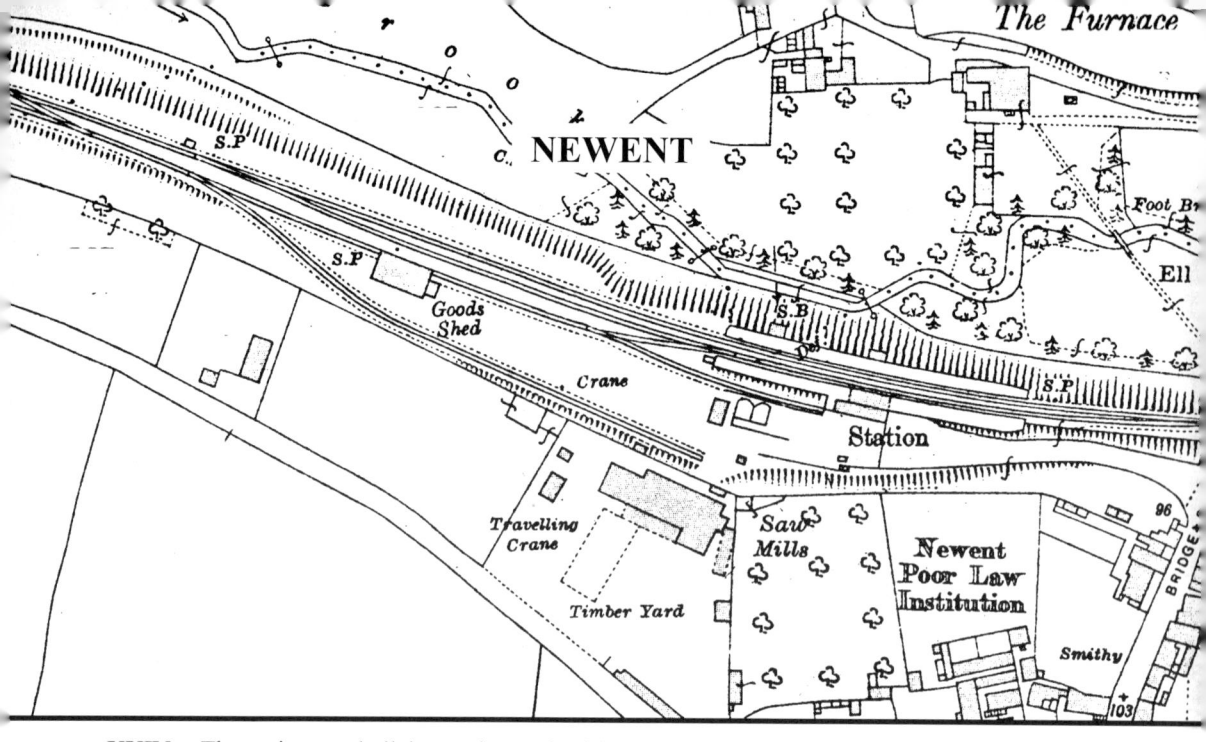

XXIV. The station was built just to the north of the town centre and the 1922 map shows the position of the 1902 signal box, which had 19 levers.

89. Looking towards Ledbury in 1919 we see the gable end of the goods shed. The town had a total of 2485 inhabitants in 1901 which increased to 3167 by 1961. Between five and seven staff were employed at the station from 1903 to 1938. (LGRP/NRM)

90. It is not possible to see that the canopy brackets carried the initials NR - Newent Railway, the original owner. The 2-6-2T is waiting to leave for Ledbury in about 1950. (M.J.Stretton coll.)

91. This and the next photograph were taken shortly before the end of passenger traffic in 1959. Behind the contemporary Morris Minor Traveller is a poster promoting "Holidays in Britain". (J.Moss/R.S.Carpenter coll.)

92. As at Dymock, goods services continued until 1st June 1964. The rodding tunnel indicates the position of the signal box on the platform until 1948. The one seen came at that time from Aston Magna - see picture 21 in *Moreton-in-Marsh to Worcester*. The station's crane was capable of lifting weights up to 5 tons. (J.Moss/R.S.Carpenter coll.)

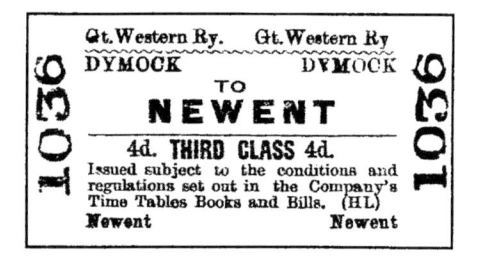

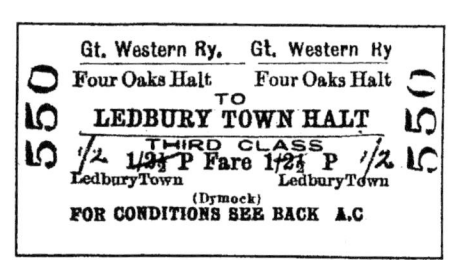

MALSWICK HALT

93. The platform came into use on 1st February 1938 and was a little over one mile from Newent on the south side of the line. (E.Wilmshurst)

94. Access was from the lane to Okle Clifford. The steps are seen in 1959, along with a 1934 Hillman Minx. (H.C.Casserley)

BARBERS BRIDGE

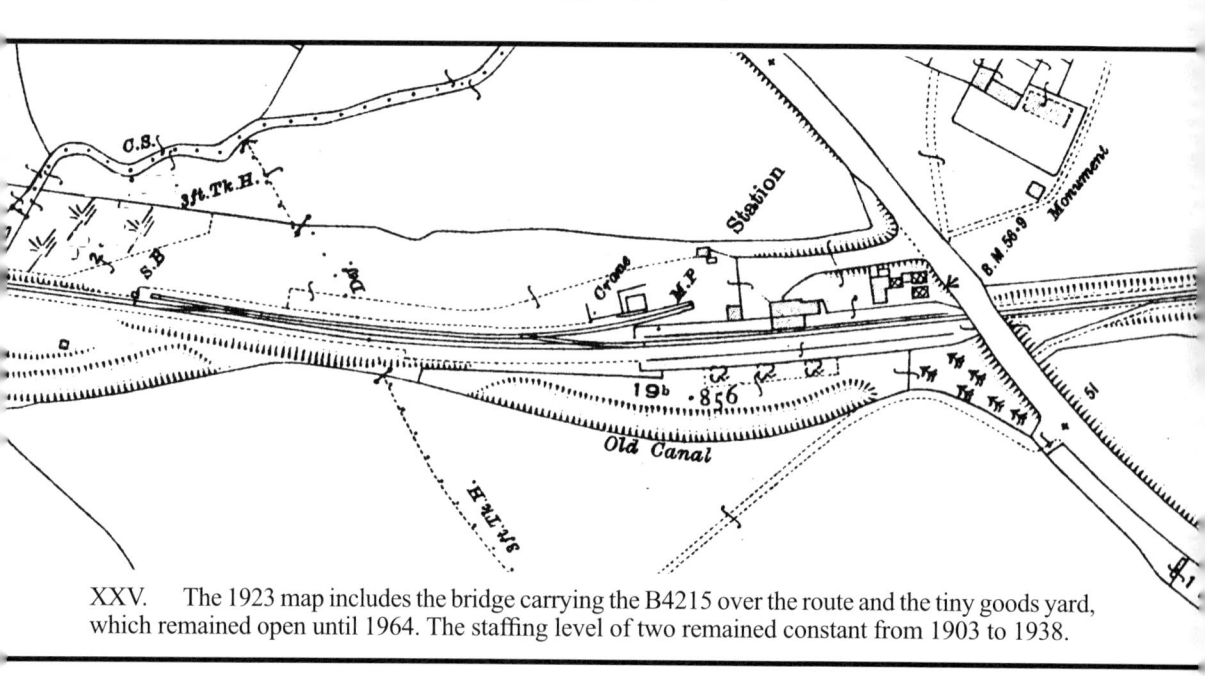

XXV. The 1923 map includes the bridge carrying the B4215 over the route and the tiny goods yard, which remained open until 1964. The staffing level of two remained constant from 1903 to 1938.

← 95. The 1919 photograph shows the bed of a passing loop, which was taken out of use in June 1898. There had been a signal box on the left until that time. Visible above the canopy is the crane which was capable of lifting up to 3 tons. (LGRP/NRM)

96. This is the view towards Gloucester in 1959. About ½ mile distant was Tibberton which had 272 residents in 1901. (J.Moss/R.S.Carpenter coll.)

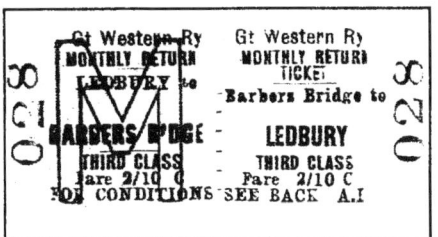

Barber's Bridge	1903	1913	1923	1933
Passenger tickets issued	8507	7743	3597	1084
Season tickets issued	*	*	56	44
Parcels forwarded 1655	5514	12885	8823	
General goods forwarded (tons)	150	602	279	141
Coal and coke received (tons)	40	99	7	191
Other minerals received (tons)	634	1245	2622	974
General goods received (tons)	160	311	754	528
Trucks of livestock handled	12	29	32	27

(* not available.)

OVER JUNCTION

97.	A snap from the rear of W19W in June 1959 shows the junction which had been realigned in September 1958 when a new bridge over the River Leadon was completed. Gloucester Cathedral is in the distance. (M.A.N.Johnston)

98.	From the other river bank we see no. 78005 on the Gloucester Docks branch on 7th April 1964. The main line from South Wales to Gloucester runs from left to right, while the branch to Newent disappears in the centre background. (M.A.N.Johnston)

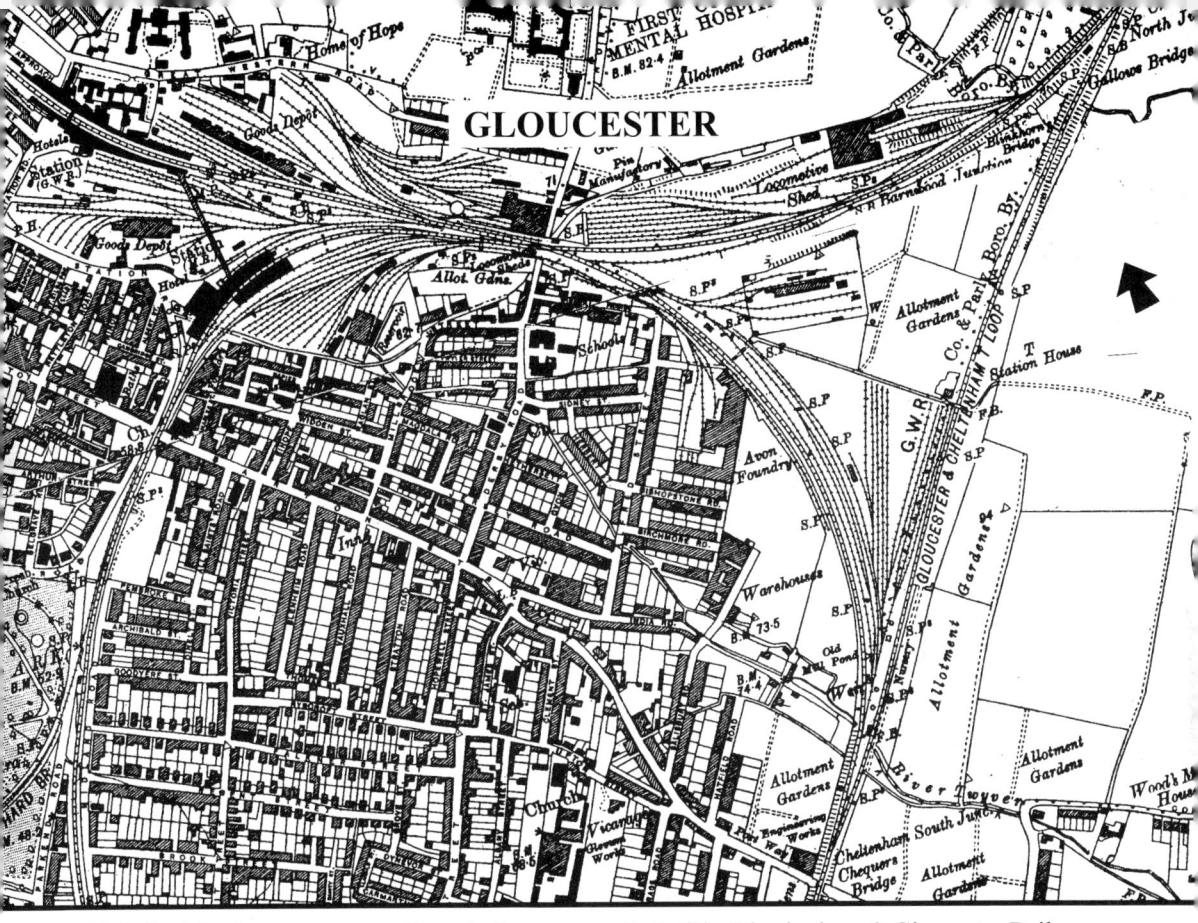

XXVI. The first passenger railway in the area was that of the Birmingham & Gloucester Railway, which terminated in the goods yard between the two stations shown top left on this 1922 survey at 6 ins to 1 mile. The upper station is on the GWR South Wales line and was named "Central" from 17th September 1951. The lower one was "Eastgate" from that date until both were considered one station on 26th May 1968. The GWR engine shed is to the left of the triangle, while the MR one is above it. A main road now bisects it at a high level.

99. The first station on this site was opened by the South Wales Railway on 19th September 1851. This eastward view is from about 1923 and includes the bay on the right which was often used by trains for Ledbury. Middle Box is on the skyline. (Stations UK)

100. No. 4698 is eastbound on 6th March 1965. Three years later, the platform on the right was used for parcels only and the footbridge was removed. The station was extensively rebuilt in 1977. (T.David/C.L.Caddy coll.)

101. The ex-GWR shed on the left was the end of the journey for loco crews and was photographed on 10th October 1965. It closed for steam traction two months later. No. 44269 is creeping round the curve from Eastgate. (T.Heavyside)

The complex story of the evolution of Gloucester's stations is included in our *Gloucester to Bristol* **album.**

5. Ashperton to Hereford
ASHPERTON

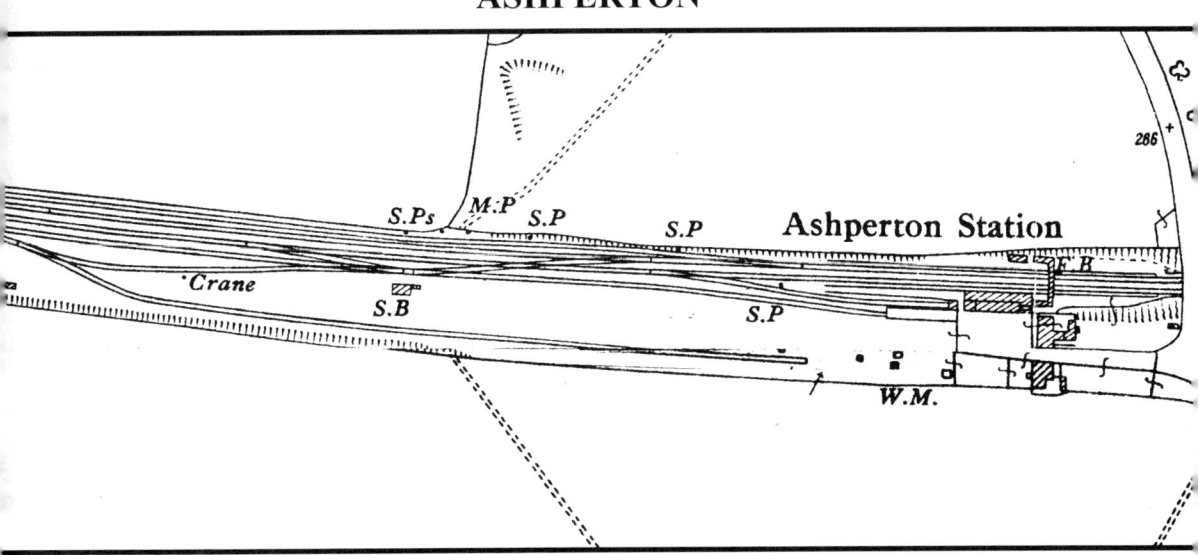

XXVII. There was little habitation in the vicinity of the station, the scattered village being more than one mile to the north. On the right of this 1928 edition is the bridge carrying the A417 north from Trumpet. The station had a small crane capable of lifting weights up to three tons.

102. A 1919 panorama from the road bridge includes parts of the 1894 buildings and the signal box, which had 25 levers and was in use until 25th October 1964. A week later, the station was designated a halt and passenger service was withdrawn on 5th April 1965. The station had six staff members from 1903 to 1931 which decreased to five until 1938. (LGRP/NRM)

103. An up express speeds through in about 1939, as a cattle wagon stands in the dock. The goods yard closed on 12th August 1963 and no structures remain today. Two miles to the east, there were goods loops in 1901-29, controlled by Rea Bridge box which had a 31-lever frame. The village was populated by 363 inhabitants in 1901. (Stations UK)

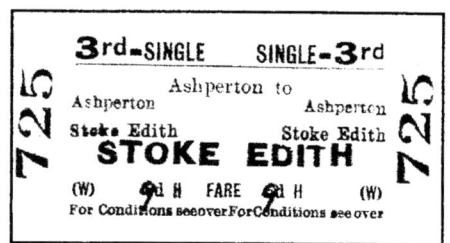

3rd-SINGLE		SINGLE-3rd
	Ashperton to	
Ashperton		Ashperton
Stoke Edith		Stoke Edith
STOKE EDITH		
(W) 9d H	FARE 9d H	(W)
For Conditions see over		For Conditions see over

725 725

Ashperton	1903	1913	1923	1933
Passenger tickets issued	16193	15108	12416	3825
Season tickets issued	*	*	45	27
Parcels forwarded	4915	5841	6009	5792
General goods forwarded (tons)	3580	2039	2909	1151
Coal and coke received (tons)	1081	938	789	772
Other minerals received (tons)	2133	9739	24444	1392
General goods received (tons)	2006	3311	1731	878
Trucks of livestock handled	31	34	56	45

(* not available.)

STOKE EDITH

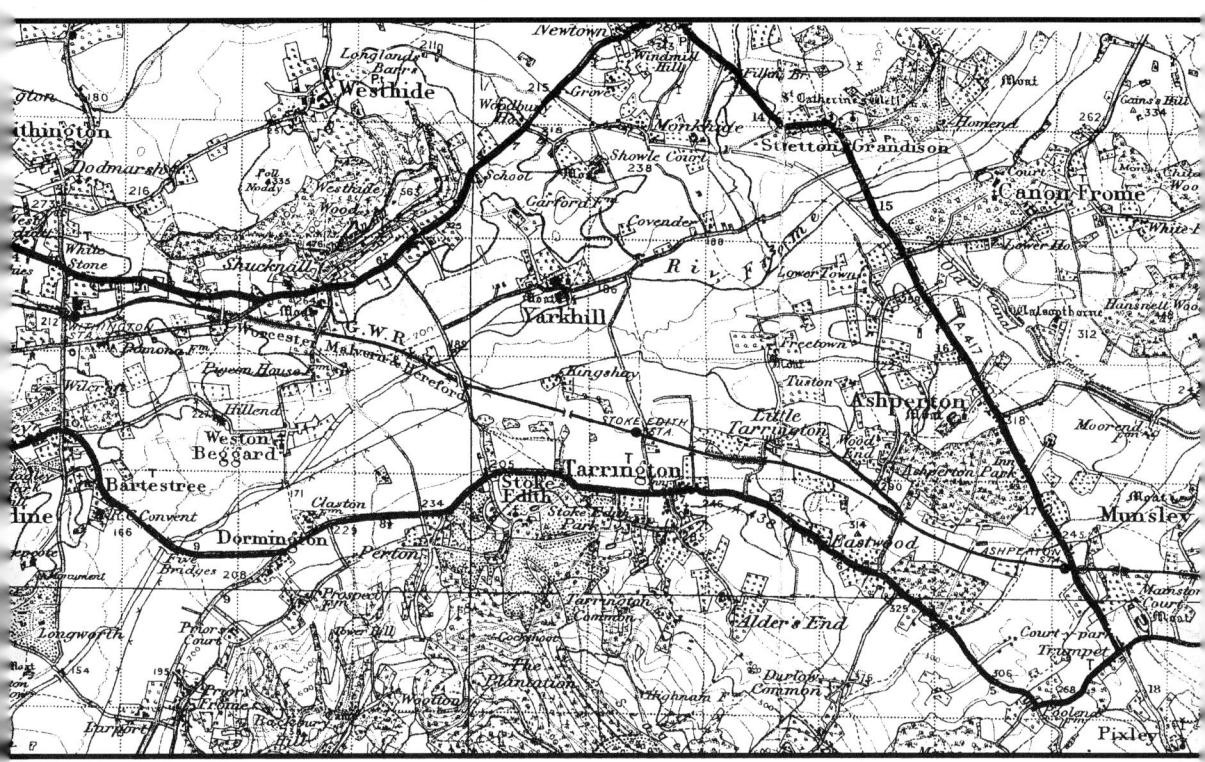

XXVIIIa The 1947 survey at 1 ins to 1 mile shows that the station was near to Tarrington. It also gives the location of the adjacent stations. Tarrington had a population of 476 which had decreased to 390 by 1961.

104.   A 1919 westward view includes an occupation bridge in the distance and part of the goods yard, which was in use until 12th August 1963. On average the station employed five staff between 1903 and 1938. (LGRP/NRM)

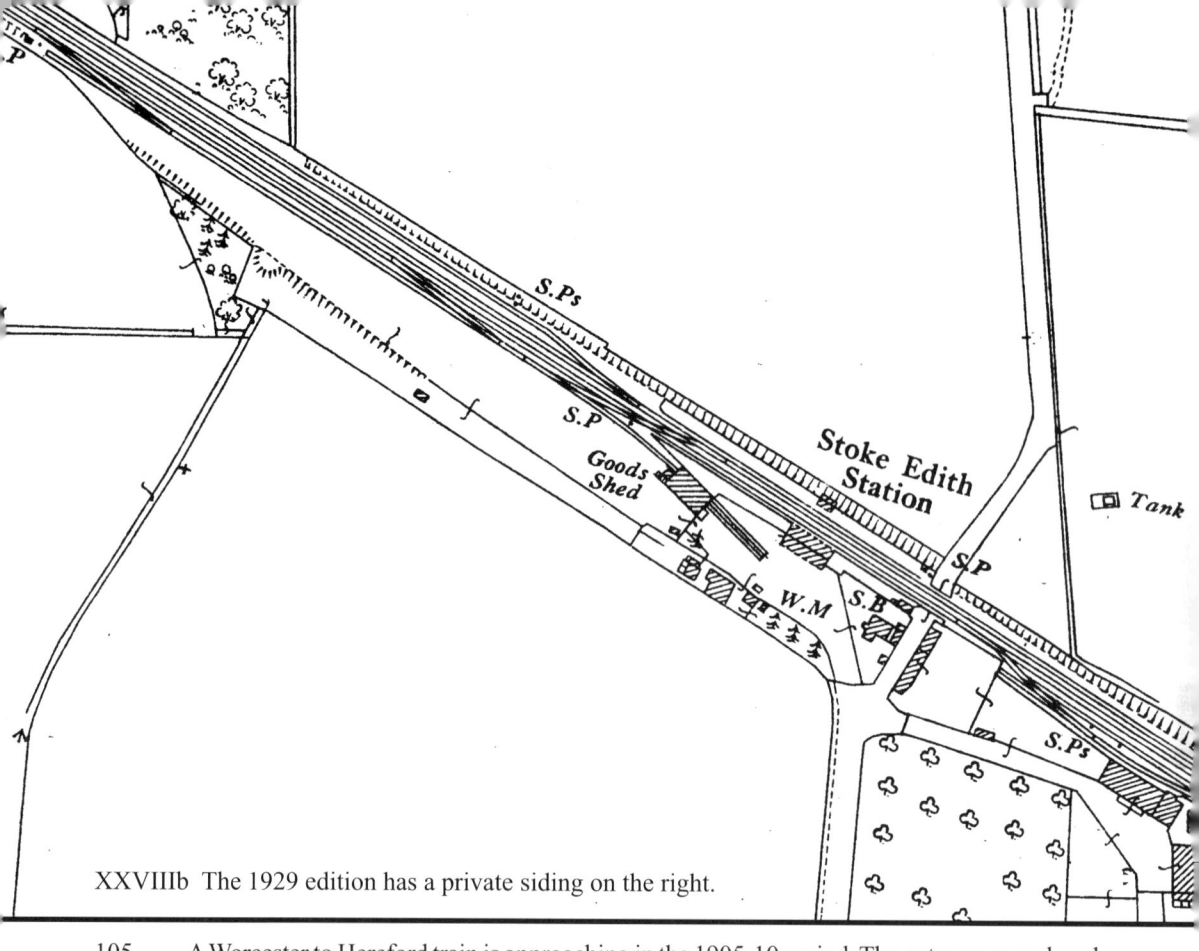

XXVIIIb The 1929 edition has a private siding on the right.

105.	A Worcester to Hereford train is approaching in the 1905-10 period. The gates were replaced by lifting barriers in February 1972. These were severely damaged by a car on 23rd April 2004, causing a delay. An apologetic guard announced that this was due to the wrong type of motorist. (Lens of Sutton coll.)

106. Passenger services were withdrawn on 5th April 1965 and the buildings seen in this 1958 photograph were demolished later. The good news is that a replica goods shed appeared in 2004, along with a bogie parcels van. (H.C.Casserley)

107. A down DMU runs through on 17th July 1965 and passes the 36-lever box which was in use until 25th November 1984. The ringed signal was for the down refuge siding. (C.L.Caddy)

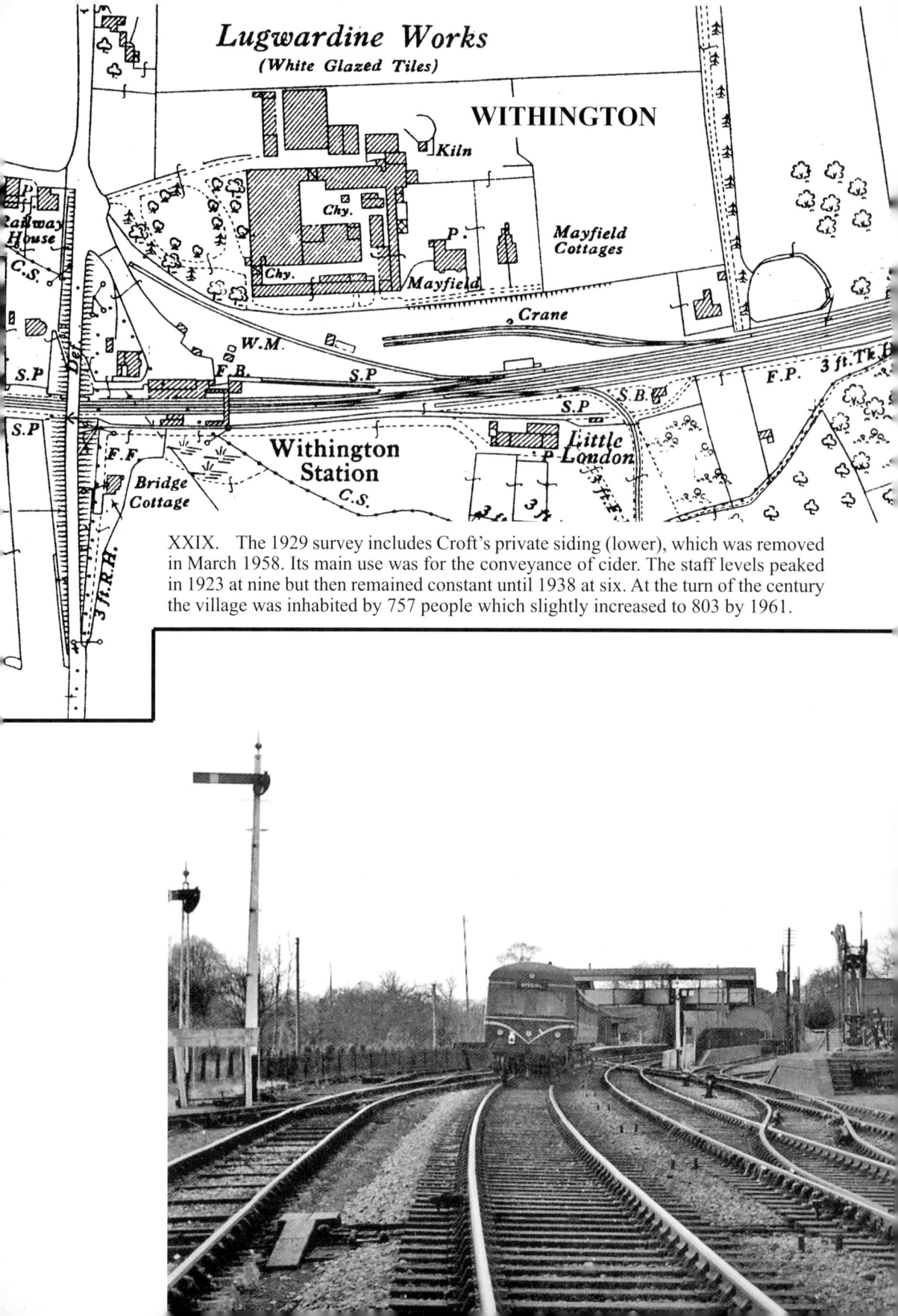

XXIX. The 1929 survey includes Croft's private siding (lower), which was removed in March 1958. Its main use was for the conveyance of cider. The staff levels peaked in 1923 at nine but then remained constant until 1938 at six. At the turn of the century the village was inhabited by 757 people which slightly increased to 803 by 1961.

108. A postcard view from the road bridge shows the second station; the first buildings were of timber construction. Passenger traffic ceased earlier than at nearby stations, the date being 2nd January 1961. Seen through the footbridge is the signal box which had 21 levers and lasted until 14th December 1964. (Lens of Sutton coll.)

109. From left to right in this February 1958 picture is the signal for the refuge siding, the outer home, a DMU on trial, the cattle dock, a one-ton crane, 0-6-0 no. 2242 and the tile works. Goods traffic ceased on 2nd November 1964. The private siding is at the foot of the signals.
(Priestley coll./Milepost 92½)

SHELWICK JUNCTION

110.   A class 40 is southbound on 24th June 1973 and is passing over the double track connections to the Worcester line. The 23-lever box closed on 11th November 1984 and no longer would coal have to be unloaded here. (T.Nicholls)

111.   A 2003 photograph features the crossover used by up trains to Worcester and emphasises the straight alignment of the Shrewsbury route. (V.Mitchell)

HEREFORD

XXX. The remainder of our journey is on the curve on the top right quarter of this 1952 6 ins scale map. This section had for a long time been a joint LNWR/GWR operation, as had the station. It was known as Barrs Court until 1893, when the GWR's Barton station (lower left) closed. This was in use for freight until 1979. North of it was the MR's Moorfields terminus for trains from Brecon, but these ran to Barrs Court from 1893, via a new curve of small radius. This was still in place in 2004, serving a power station, two industrial premises and Bulmer's cider works. The MR engine shed is marked, although this had not been used since 1924.

112. Our journey ends at the island platform, seen here in about 1923. Trains from Gloucester via Ross had been broad gauge until 1869 and a separate engine shed was provided behind the camera. It was later used as a carriage shed, the main loco depot being established at Barton. The turntable is shown on the map. (Stations UK)

113. A southward view from the same period features the two through lines. Empty stock often stood on them as through freight services usually ran via Barton, a more direct route. (Stations UK)

114. The first permanent station on this site was completed in 1855 and was replaced by this fine structure during major improvements in 1878-83. The first station had a large shed containing bay platforms end to end nearest the building and a through line on the east side. The latter was mixed gauge, the southern bay was broad and the northern one standard. This is a 1958 photo. (H.C.Casserley)

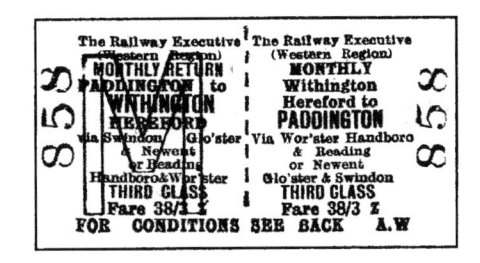

115. A northward panorama from September 1962 includes no. 5939 *Tangley Hall* in the up bay, with a DMU approaching the island platform. The up goods shed of 1855 is featured along with the two footbridges that linked it with a similar building on the down side. They were the northern limit of the mixed gauge tracks. A shunting engine was provided for both yards, day and night, until the 1950s. (F.Hornby)

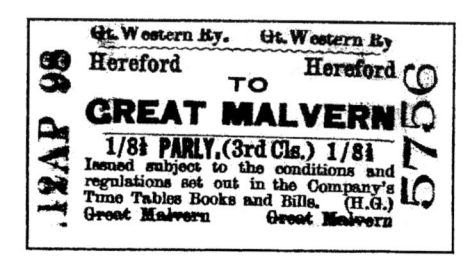

116. This is a 1967 eastward view of the 1893 Brecon Curve, with the line from Shelwick Junction on the left. We are looking at the back of Brecon Curve Junction box, which had 80 levers. North of it was Barrs Court Junction box which housed a 28-lever frame. (M.A.N.Johnston)

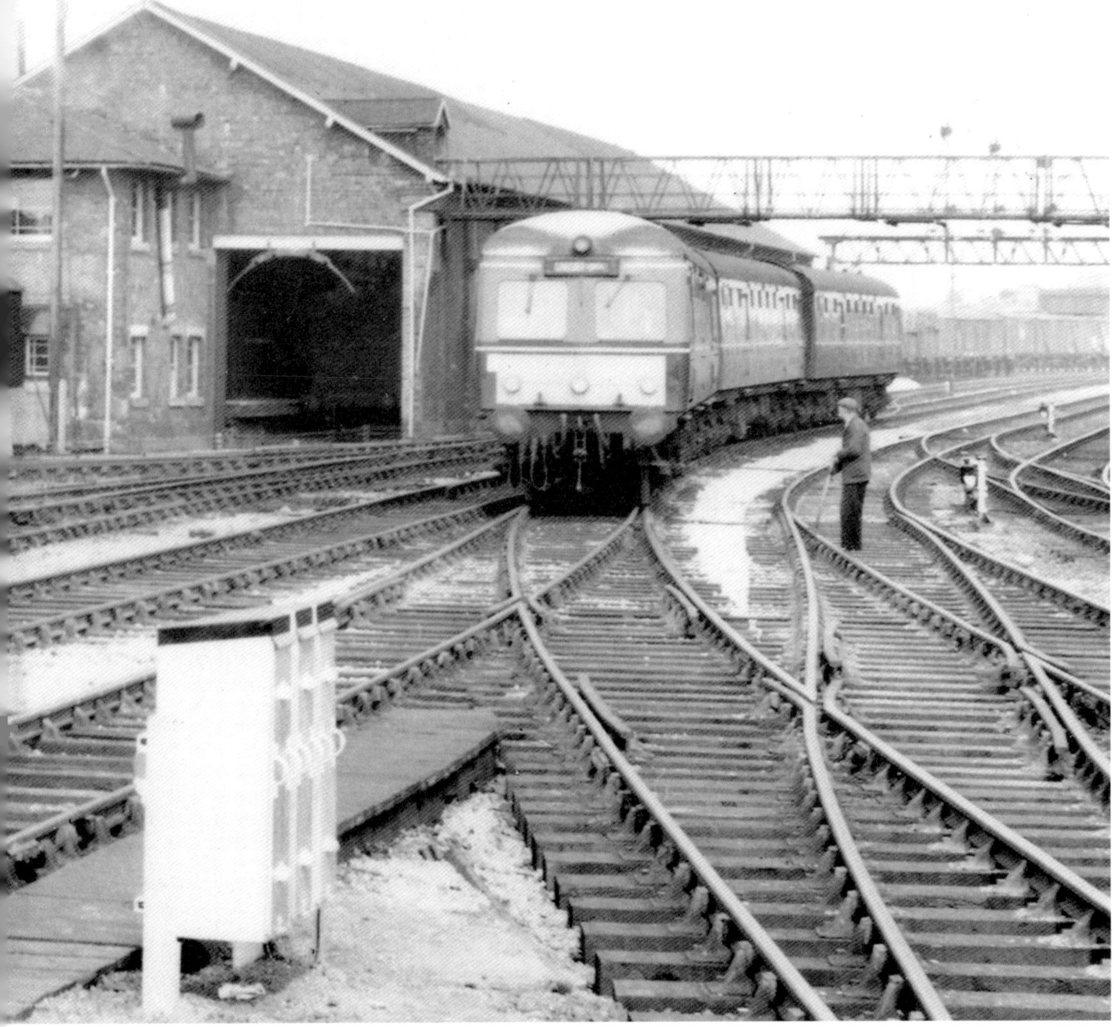

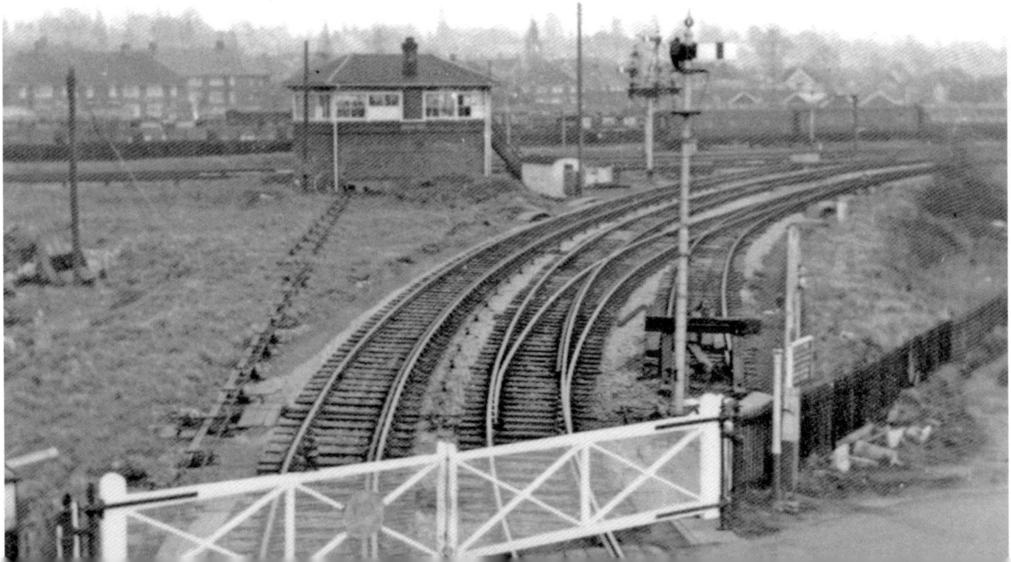

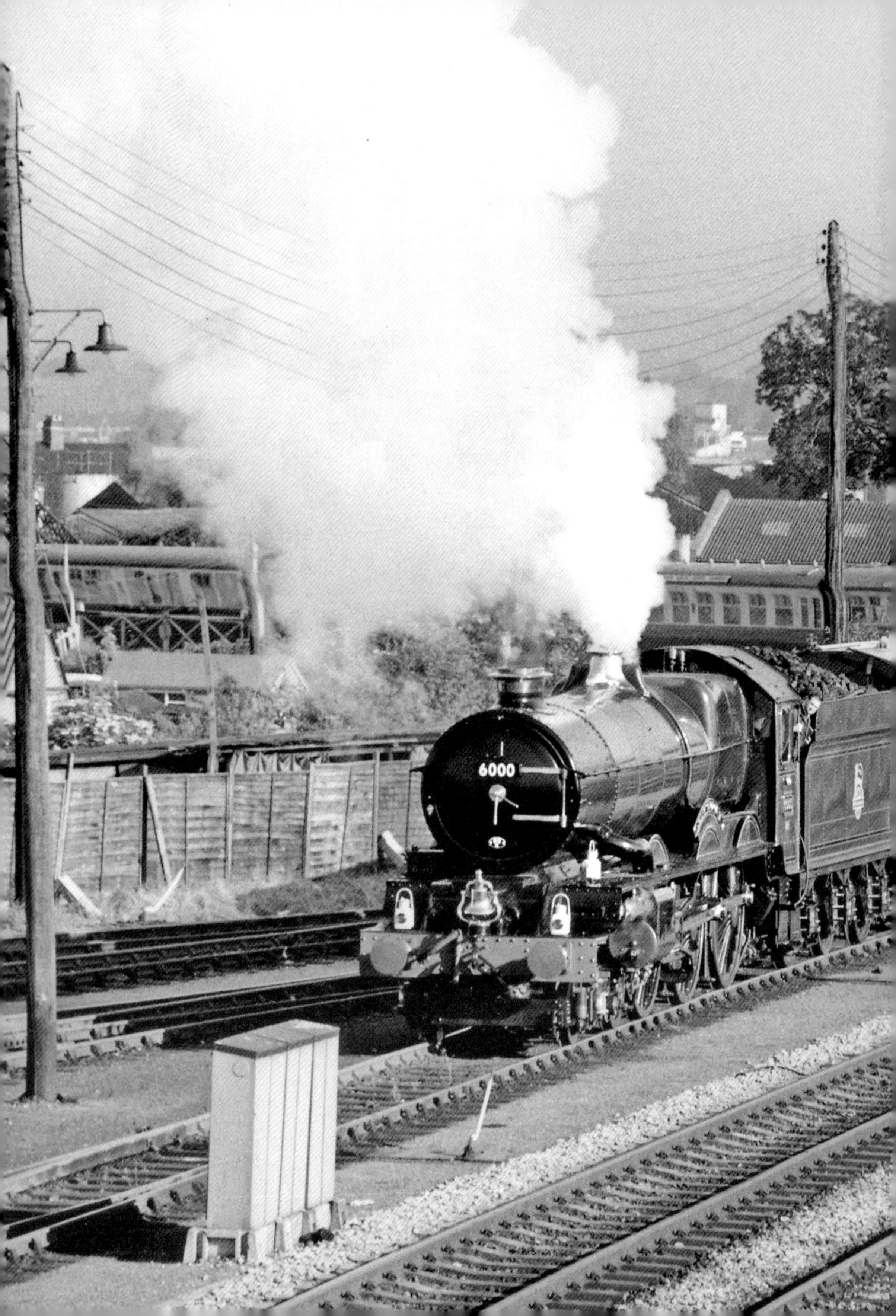
6000

117. Bulmers publicised their cider by means of their own 5-coach converted Pullman train and no. 6000 *King George V*, which was leased until 1988. It is seen on 3rd July 1977 leaving the Brecon Curve on the loco's 50th anniversary run, with stock from the Severn Valley Railway. The steam centre existed from 1968 until 31st May 1993. (T.Heavyside)

118.   The Brecon Curve is on the left as no. 47266 arrives from the north with a parcels train on 24th April 1982. The site on the right was occupied by an LMS engine shed (ex-LNWR) until 1938. The turntable remained for another 20 years or so. (T.Heavyside)

119.   The buildings were listed in 1973 and are seen on 31st July 1993 as the 16.29 is about to depart for Birmingham. It is formed of "Sprinter" unit no. 150124. (N.W.Sprinks)

120. The bay platform was added in 1893 for use by MR trains to Brecon, some continuing to Swansea. No. 60097 was recorded with a load of steel from South Wales on 26th March 2003. In the centre is Hereford's remaining signal box, which had its 69 levers reduced to 60 when a panel was added in November 1984. It was earlier known as "Aylstone Hill". There was still some variety to be enjoyed by the railway student in this delightful part of Britain. (V.Mitchell)

MP Middleton Press

Easebourne Lane, Midhurst
West Sussex. GU29 9AZ

OOP Out of Print - Please check current availability **BROCHURE AVAILABLE SHOWING NEW TITLES**
Tel:01730 813169   www.middletonpress.com   email:middletonpress.co.uk

A
Abergavenny to Merthyr C 91 5
Aldgate & Stepney Tramways B 70 7
Allhallows - Branch Line to A 62 2
Alton - Branch Lines to A 11 8
Andover to Southampton A 82 7
Ascot - Branch Lines around A 64 9
Ashburton - Branch Line to B 95 2
Ashford - Steam to Eurostar B 67 7
Ashford to Dover A 48 7
Austrian Narrow Gauge D 04 7

B
Banbury to Birmingham D 27 6
Barking to Southend C 80 X
Barnet & Finchley Tramways B 93 6
Basingstoke to Salisbury A 89 4
Bath Green Park to Bristol C 36 2
Bath to Evercreech Junction A 60 6
Bath Tramways B 34 4
Battle over Portsmouth 1940 A 29 0
Battle over Sussex 1940 A 79 7
Bedford to Wellingborough D 31 4
Betwixt Petersfield & Midhurst A 94 0
Blitz over Sussex 1941-42 B 35 9
Bodmin - Branch Lines around B 83 9
Bognor at War 1939-45 B 59 6
Bombers over Sussex 1943-45 B 51 0
Bournemouth & Poole Trys B 47 2 OOP
Bournemouth to Evercreech Jn A 46 0
Bournemouth to Weymouth A 57 6
Bournemouth Trolleybuses C 10 9
Bradford Trolleybuses D 19 5
Brecon to Newport D 16 0
Brickmaking in Sussex B 19 7
Brightons Tramways B 02 2
Brighton to Eastbourne A 16 9
Brighton to Worthing A 03 7
Bristols Tramways B 57 X
Bristol to Taunton D 03 9
Bromley South to Rochester B 23 5 OOP
Bude - Branch Line to B 29 4
Burnham to Evercreech Jn A 68 1
Burton & Ashby Tramways C 51 6

C
Camberwell & West Norwood TW B 22 7
Canterbury - Branch Lines around B 58 8
Caterham & Tattenham Corner B 25 1
Changing Midhurst C 15 X
Chard and Yeovil - BLs around C 30 3
Charing Cross to Dartford A 75 4
Charing Cross to Orpington A 96 7
Cheddar - Branch Line to B 90 1
Cheltenham to Andover C 43 5
Chesterfield Tramways D 37 3
Chichester to Portsmouth A 14 2 OOP
Clapham & Streatham Tramways B 97 9
Clapham Junction - 50 yrs C 06 0
Clapham Junction to Beckenham Jn B 36 7
Clevedon & Portishead - BLs to D 18 7
Collectors Trains, Trolleys & Trams D 29 2
Crawley to Littlehampton A 34 7
Cromer - Branch Lines around C 26 5
Croydons Tramways B 42 1
Croydons Trolleybuses B 73 1
Croydon to East Grinstead B 48 0
Crystal Palace (HL) & Catford Loop A 87 8

D
Darlington Trolleybuses D 33 0
Dartford to Sittingbourne B 34 0
Derby Tramways D 17 9
Derby Trolleybuses C 72 9
Derwent Valley - Branch Line to the D 06 3
Didcot to Banbury D 02 0
Didcot to Swindon C 84 2
Didcot to Winchester C 13 3
Douglas to Peel C 88 5
Douglas to Port Erin C 55 9
Douglas to Ramsey D 39 X
Dover's Tramways B 24 3
Dover to Ramsgate A 78 9

E
Ealing to Slough C 42 7
Eastbourne to Hastings A 27 4 OOP
East Croydon to Three Bridges A 53 3
East Grinstead - Branch Lines to A 07 X
East Ham & West Ham Tramways B 52 9
East Kent Light Railway A 61 4
East London - Branch Lines of C 44 3
East London Line B 80 4
East Ridings Secret Resistance D 21 7
Edgware & Willesden Tramways C 18 4
Effingham Junction - BLs around A 74 6
Eltham & Woolwich Tramways B 74 X
Ely to Kings Lynn C 53 2
Ely to Norwich C 90 7
Embankment & Waterloo Tramways B 41 3
Enfield & Wood Green Trys C 03 6 OOP
Enfield Town & Palace Gates - BL to D 32 2
Epsom to Horsham A 30 4
Euston to Harrow & Wealdstone C 89 3
Exeter & Taunton Tramways B 32 4
Exeter to Barnstaple B 15 4
Exeter to Newton Abbot C 49 4
Exeter to Tavistock B 69 3
Exmouth - Branch Lines to B 00 6 OOP

F
Fairford - Branch Line to A 52 5
Falmouth, Helston & St. Ives - BL to C 74 5
Fareham to Salisbury A 67 3
Faversham to Dover B 05 7 OOP
Felixstowe & Aldeburgh - BL to D 20 9
Fenchurch Street to Barking C 20 6
Festiniog - 50 yrs of change C 83 4
Festiniog in the Fifties B 68 5
Festiniog in the Sixties B 91 X
Finsbury Park to Alexandra Palace C 02 8
Frome to Bristol B 77 4
Fulwell - Trams, Trolleys & Buses D 11 X

G
Garraway Father & Son A 20 7 OOP
Gloucester to Bristol D 35 7
Gosport & Horndean Trys B 92 8 OOP
Gosport - Branch Lines around A 36 3
Great Yarmouth Tramways D 13 6
Greenwich & Dartford Tramways B 14 6
Guildford to Redhill A 63 0

H
Hammersmith & Hounslow Trys C 33 8
Hampshire Narrow Gauge D 36 5
Hampshire Waterways A 84 3 OOP
Hampstead & Highgate Tramways B 53 7
Harrow to Watford D 59 4
Hastings to Ashford A 37 1 OOP
Hastings Tramways B 18 9
Hastings Trolleybuses B 81 2
Hawkhurst - Branch Line to A 66 5
Hayling - Branch Line to A 12 6
Haywards Heath to Seaford A 28 2 OOP
Henley, Windsor & Marlow - BL to C77 X
Hitchin to Peterborough D 07 1
Holborn & Finsbury Tramways B 79 0
Holborn Viaduct to Lewisham A 81 9
Horsham - Branch Lines to A 02 9
Huddersfield Trolleybuses C 92 3
Hull Trolleybuses D 24 1
Huntingdon - Branch Lines around A 93 2

I
Ilford & Barking Tramways B 61 8
Ilford to Shenfield C 97 4
Ilfracombe - Branch Line to B 21 9
Industrial Rlys of the South East A 09 6
Ipswich to Saxmundham C 41 9
Isle of Wight Lines - 50 yrs C 12 5

K
Kent & East Sussex Waterways A 72 X
Kent Narrow Gauge C 45 1
Kingsbridge - Branch Line to C 98 2
Kingston & Hounslow Loops A 83 5
Kingston & Wimbledon Tramways B 56 1
Kingswear - Branch Line to C 17 6

L
Lambourn - Branch Line to C 70 2
Launceston & Princetown - BL to C 19 2
Lewisham & Catford Tramways B 26 X
Lewisham to Dartford A 92 4 OOP
Lines around Wimbledon B 75 8
Liverpool Street to Chingford D 01 2
Liverpool Street to Ilford C 34 6

Liverpool Tramways - Eastern C 04 4
Liverpool Tramways - Northern C 46 X
Liverpool Tramways - Southern C 23 0
London Bridge to Addiscombe B 20 0
London Bridge to East Croydon A 58 4
London Chatham & Dover Rly A 88 6
London Termini - Past and Proposed D 00 4
London to Portsmouth Waterways B 43 X
Longmoor - Branch Lines to A 41 X
Looe - Branch Line to C 22 2
Lyme Regis - Branch Line to A 45 2
Lynton - Branch Line to B 04 9

M
Maidstone & Chatham Tramways B 40 5
Maidstone Trolleybuses C 00 1 OOP
March - Branch Lines around B 09 X
Margate & Ramsgate Tramways C 52 4
Midhurst - Branch Lines around A 49 5
Midhurst - Branch Lines to A 01 0 OOP
Military Defence of West Sussex A 23 1
Military Signals, South Coast C 54 0
Minehead - Branch Line to A 80 0
Mitcham Junction Lines B 01 4
Mitchell & company C 59 1 OOP
Moreton-in-Marsh to Worcester D 26 8
Moretonhampstead - Branch Line to C 27 3

N
Newbury to Westbury C 66 4
Newport - Branch Lines to A 26 6
Newquay - Branch Lines to C 71 0
Newton Abbot to Plymouth C 60 5
Northern France Narrow Gauge C 75 3
North Kent Tramways B 44 8
North London Line B 94 4
North Woolwich - BLs around C 65 6
Norwich Tramways C 40 0

O
Orpington to Tonbridge B 03 0
Oxford to Moreton-in-Marsh D 15 2

P
Paddington to Ealing C 37 0
Paddington to Princes Risborough C 81 8
Padstow - Branch Line to B 54 5
Plymouth - BLs around B 98 7
Plymouth to St. Austell C 63 X
Porthmadog 1954-94 - BL around B 31 6
Porthmadog to Blaenau B 50 2 OOP
Portmadoc 1923-46 - BL around B 13 8
Portsmouths Tramways B 72 3 OOP
Portsmouth to Southampton A 31 2
Portsmouth Trolleybuses C 73 7
Princes Risborough - Branch Lines to D 05 5
Princes Risborough to Banbury C 85 0

R
Railways to Victory C 16 8
Reading to Basingstoke B 27 8
Reading to Didcot C 79 6
Reading to Guildford A 47 9
Reading Tramways B 87 1
Reading Trolleybuses C 05 2
Redhill to Ashford A 73 8
Return to Blaenau 1970-82 C 64 8
Roman Roads of Surrey C 61 3
Roman Roads of Sussex C 48 6
Romneyrail C 32 X
Ryde to Ventnor A 19 3

S
Salisbury to Westbury B 39 1
Salisbury to Yeovil B 06 5
Saxmundham to Yarmouth C 69 9
Seaton & Eastbourne T/Ws B 76 6 OOP
Seaton & Sidmouth - Branch Lines to A 95 9
Secret Sussex Resistance B 82 0
SECR Centenary album C 11 7
Selsey - Branch Line to A 04 5 OOP
Sheerness - Branch Lines around B 16 2
Shepherds Bush to Uxbridge T/Ws C 28 1
Shrewsbury - Branch Line to A 86 X
Sierra Leone Narrow Gauge D 28 4
Sittingbourne to Ramsgate A 90 8
Slough to Newbury C 56 7
Southamptons Tramways B 33 2 OOP
Southampton to Bournemouth A 42 8
Southend-on-Sea Tramways B 28 6

Southern France Narrow Gauge C 47 8
Southwark & Deptford Tramways B 38 3
Southwold - Branch Line to A 15 0
South Eastern & Chatham Railways C 08 7
South London Line B 46 4
South London Tramways 1903-33 D 10 1
St. Albans to Bedford D 08 X
St. Austell to Penzance C 67 2
St. Pancras to St. Albans C 78 8
Stamford Hill Tramways B 85 5
Steaming through Cornwall B 30 8
Steaming through Kent A 13 4
Steaming through the Isle of Wight A 56 8
Steaming through West Hants A 69 X
Stratford-upon-Avon to Cheltenham C 25 7
Strood to Paddock Wood B 12 5
Surrey Home Guard C 57 5
Surrey Narrow Gauge C 87 7
Surrey Waterways A 51 7 OOP
Sussex Home Guard C 24 9
Sussex Narrow Gauge C 68 0
Sussex Shipping Sail, Steam & Motor D 23 ...
Swanage revised 1999 - BL to A 33 9 OOP
Swanley to Ashford B 45 6
Swindon to Bristol C 96 6
Swindon to Newport D 30 6
Swiss Narrow Gauge C 94 X

T
Talyllyn - 50 years C 39 7
Taunton to Barnstaple B 60 X 3
Taunton to Exeter C 82 6
Tavistock to Plymouth B 88 X
Tenterden - Branch Line to A 21 5
Thanet's Tramways B 11 1 OOP
Three Bridges to Brighton A 35 5
Tilbury Loop C 86 9
Tiverton - Branch Lines around C 62 1
Tonbridge to Hastings A 44 4
Torrington - Branch Lines to B 37 5
Tunbridge Wells - Branch Lines to A 32 0
Twickenham & Kingston Trys C 35 4
Two-Foot Gauge Survivors C 21 4 OOP

U
Upwell - Branch Line to B 64 2

V
Victoria & Lambeth Tramways B 49 9
Victoria to Bromley South A 98 3
Victoria to East Croydon A 40 1
Vivarais C 31 1

W
Walthamstow & Leyton Tramways B 65 0
Waltham Cross & Edmonton Trys C 07 9
Wandsworth & Battersea Tramways B 63 4
Wantage - Branch Line to D 25 X
Wareham to Swanage - 50 yrs D 09 8
War on the Line A 10 X
Waterloo to Windsor A 54 1
Waterloo to Woking A 38 X
Wenford Bridge to Fowey C 09 5
Westbury to Bath B 55 3
Westbury to Taunton C 76 1
West Croydon to Epsom B 08 1
West London - Branch Lines of C 50 8
West London Line B 84 7
West Sussex Waterways A 24 X
West Wiltshire - Branch Lines of D 12 8
Weymouth - Branch Lines around A 65 7
Willesden Junction to Richmond B 71 5
Wimbledon to Beckenham C 58 3
Wimbledon to Epsom B 62 6
Wimborne - Branch Lines around A 97 5
Wisbech - Branch Lines around C 01 X
Wisbech 1800-1901 C 93 1
Woking to Alton A 59 2
Woking to Portsmouth A 25 8
Woking to Southampton A 55 X
Woolwich & Dartford TrolleyB B 66 9 OOP
Worcester to Hereford D 38 1
Worthing to Chichester A 06 1 OOP

Y
Yeovil - 50 yrs change C 38 9
Yeovil to Dorchester A 76 2
Yeovil to Exeter A 91 6

96